MILLER'S
Antiques Checklist
ART DECO

Consultant: Eric Knowles

General Editors:
Judith and Martin Miller

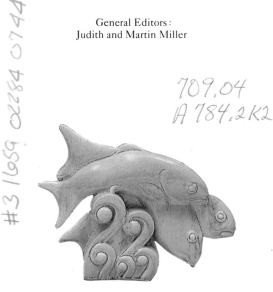

MILLER'S ANTIQUES CHECKLIST: ART DECO

Consultant: Eric Knowles

First published in Great Britain in 1991 by Miller's,
a division of Mitchell Beazley,
both imprints of Octopus Publishing Group Ltd.
2–4 Heron Quays
Docklands
London E14 4JP

Miller's is a registered trademark of Octopus Publishing Group Ltd.

Series Editor	Frances Gertler
Series Art Editor	Nigel O'Gorman
Art Editor	Christopher Howson
Illustrators	Karen Cochrane
	John Hutchinson
Editorial Assistants	Katie Martin-Doyle
	Jaspal Bhangra
Design Assistant	Elaine Hewson
Typesetter	Kerrie Hinchon
Production	Barbara Hind
	Ted Timberlake

©1991 Octopus Publishing Group Ltd.
Reprinted 1994, 1995, 1996, 1997, 1998, 1999
This edition published 2000

A CIP catalogue record for this book is available
from the British Library

ISBN 1 84000 280 8

Set in Caslon 540, Caslon 224 bold and Caslon 3
Produced by Toppan Printing Co., (HK) Ltd.
Printed and bound in China

Jacket: *Opalescent glass figurine by Edmund Etling Et Cie c.1925*

CONTENTS

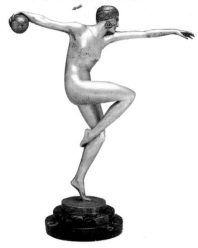

CERAMICS

SCULPTURE

PRINTS AND POSTERS

METALWORK

SILVER AND JEWELRY

RUGS

GLOSSARY 180

HOW TO USE THIS BOOK

When I first started collecting antiques although there were many informative books on the subject I still felt hesitant when it came to actually buying an antique. What I really wanted to do was interrogate the piece – to find out what it was and whether it was genuine.

The *Art Deco* Checklist will show you how to assess a piece as an expert would, and provides checklists of questions you should ask before making a purchase. The answer to most (if not all) of the questions should be "yes", but there are always exceptions to the rule: if in doubt, seek expert guidance.

The book is divided into collecting categories, each with an introduction and, for those with a limited budget, special sections on inexpensive pieces which in many cases are considered "minor" only because they are not by leading craftsmen. At the back of the book are a glossary, bibliography and a list of principal makers and retailers and their marks.

Treat the book as a knowledgeable companion, and soon you will find that antique collecting is a matter of experience, and of knowing how to ask the right questions.

JUDITH MILLER

Each double-page spread looks at the work of an individual craftsman or factory.

The first page shows a carefully chosen representative item of a type that can usually be found at antique stores or auction houses (rather than only in museums).

The caption gives the date and dimensions of the piece shown, and a code for the price range of this type of article.

A checklist of questions gives you the key to recognizing, dating and authenticating antique pieces of the type shown.

THE DAUM

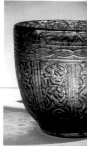

A Daum glass bo...
... 1915, h 8" suffixes...

Identification checklist for Daum e...
1. Does the piece make use of all-c...
2. Is it signed, probably on the foo...
3. Is the surface grainy and uneven...
4. Is the decoration abstract?
5. Is the form fairly heavy and thic... robust impression?

Value point
The hand-made pieces of the early Art Deco years fetch more than those from the industrial period of the later 20s and 30s.

Authenticity
Fakers have yet to turn their attention to Daum glass. Wares are usually signed (see **The Daum Factory**, *opposite*).

Condition
The rims of Daum glass are usually gently rounded. A sharp edge might indicate that a chip has been removed using a polishing wheel. This practice might also be detected by examining the proportions.
46

Fake
Few f...
marke...
acid-c...
regard...
impor...
forms...
smalle...
inferie...

Colo...
Daum...
and d...
comm...
* smo...
* gree...
* ame...
* yello...
* turq...

Information helps you to detect fakes, copies and reproductions.

The second page shows you
what details to look for.

Useful background information
is provided about the craftsman
or factory.

The Daum Factory (French;
established 1875).
During the Art Nouveau period
(1890-1914) this leading
glassworks produced a large
quantity of cameo, or overlay,
glass, with the naturalistic motifs
typical of the period. During the
1920s and 30s the output
consisted of mainly etched glass,
which soon superseded cameo
glass in popularity, although the
firm continued to make cameo
glass throughout the period.
Following closure during the First
World War, the factory reopened
in 1919 under Paul Daum.
  The Daum glassworks embraced
Art Deco with enthusiasm during
the 1920s, and their lamps, bowls
and large decorative vases took an
innovative direction. Heavy acid-
etched wares with deep
decoration predominated. The
most popular colours were smoky
grey, turquoise, yellow and sea
green. Clear glass was also used
occasionally. The emphasis was
on decorative ornament and
irregular, frosted, light-diffusing
granular surfaces. Some of these
wares were reminiscent of the
designs of Marinot (see pp. 44-5).
Alternatively, matt and polished
surfaces were combined. Decoration,
either geometric or floral, tends to
be freeform although it may be
more formalized, as in the bowl
shown here. Most pieces are
wheel-engraved with the words
"Daum, Nancy" and the insignia,
the cross of Lorraine (which was
also used by other Nancy
glassworks), but wares do not
carry the names or initials of
individual designers.
  Most of the glass of the period is
thick-walled and heavy in form.
Being robust, it has generally
survived well.

Second only to the vases, lamps
were an important part of the
factory's output during this
period. This etched glass lamp
with a frosted white ground and
an acid-etched geometric design,
is typical. Daum made glass lamps
and also supplied glass shades for
other lamps, most notably for the
wrought-iron bases produced by
Edgar Brandt (see pp. 144-5).
Heavyweight lead glass was used
for hanging and standard lamps.
These items were mass-
produced, but copied the labour-
intensive hand-decorated work of
such craftsmen as Décorchement
and Argy-Rousseau. From a
distance this could be taken for
pâte de cristal. Many of the lamps
were mushroom shaped and
amber or amethyst with a mottled
perimeter in contrasting colours.
Surfaces were matt. They usually
carry a wheel- or acid-etched
signature.
* The heavy forms of acid-etched
glass produced by Lalique during
the 1970s and 30s are similar to
those of Daum.

Further photographs
and/or line drawings
show:
*.items in a different
style by the same
craftsman or factory
* similar, but perhaps
less valuable wares
that may be mistaken
for the more
collectable type
* common variations
on the piece shown in
the main picture
* similar wares by
other craftsmen
* the range of shapes
or decorative motifs
associated with a
particular factory or
period.

Marks, signatures and
serial numbers are
explained.

Other typical Daum lamps

Examining Daum glass lamps
If possible, remove the metal mount and examine the neck of the base
under a strong light – when the lamp is on the heat can cause the glass
to crack. Internal cracks may not be readily apparent.

47

Hints and tips help you to assess
factors that affect value – for
example, condition and availability.

The codes are as follows:

A £10,000+ ($15,000+)   E £500-1,000 ($750-1,500)
B £5-10,000 ($7,500-15,000)   F £200-500 ($300-750)
C £2-5,000 ($3-7,500)   G £100-200 ($150-300)
D £1-2,000 ($1,500- 3000)

INTRODUCTION

Throughout the 1950s and 60s many dealers and collectors considered little if anything of the post-1830 period to be of any merit. With the growing interest worldwide in antiques, the availability of 18th and 19th century pieces began to dwindle. This led to an increasing demand for artefacts first from the reign of William IV and then from the Victorian period. Eventually, during the 1960s and early 70s, collectors turned their attention to Art Nouveau, and a few years later they began to recognize the originality of furniture and decorative art objects from the 1920s and 30s, collectively known as Art Deco.

Pieces from the Art Deco period are sought after not only for their high quality of craftsmanship and inventive forms, but also because they evoke the giddy Twenties – the era of jazz and Hollywood – and the Thirties. New items appeared that reflected the changing lifestyles – such as cocktail glasses and car mascots. Many such pieces display in their decoration a preoccupation with speed and travel. Women came into their own as subjects during this period and are often depicted in decidedly "modern" clothing or situations – for example, smoking or participating in sports, both activities that would have seemed almost inconceivable only a few years earlier.

The term Art Deco encompasses two very different styles – the Traditional and the Modern. The Traditionalists, led by the Frenchmen Jacques-Émile Ruhlmann and Jean Dunand, adapted and embellished 18th century designs, using exotic woods and materials, and with an emphasis on comfort. The Modernists, such as Ludwig Mies van der Rohe and the British firm of Isokon, advocated clean profiles, machine-made materials and mass production. Although the Traditionalist pieces mostly belong to the 1920s and the Modernist to the 30s, both styles are evident throughout the period.

Craftsman-made pieces, such as the glasswares of Maurice Marinot and the jewelry of Jean Fouquet, are hard to come by and can be prohibitively expensive for many collectors. However, the mass-produced hand-finished wares are more readily available and more affordable.

The *Art Deco Checklist* is a complete sourcebook of the major craftsmen, factories and styles of the period. Its purpose is to teach how to recognize and assess individual pieces, and provide useful background information on the makers and media. The rest of the work you must do yourself. There is no substitute for first-hand experience: attend auctions and study pieces in museums. Collecting is a matter of experience and confidence. With the help of this book you will quickly find yourself able to make informed judgements, and with this will come the excitement and fun of knowledgeable collecting.

ERIC KNOWLES

THE PARIS EXHIBITION AND THE LINER, S. S. NORMANDIE

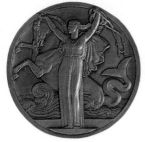

Paris Exhibition medal

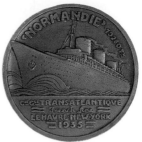

S. S. Normandie *medal*

The Art Deco style is firmly associated with two "showcases" – the Paris Exhibition and the liner *S. S. Normandie*, launched in 1935.

The Paris Exhibition – the *Exposition des Arts Decoratifs et Industriels Modernes* – took place in 1925. It was originally intended to be held some ten years earlier, but was delayed because of the War. Encouraged by the French government who were hoping it would generate trade, the Exhibition was a huge extravaganza. Designers from other countries, in particular the United States and to a lesser extent Britain, were inspired by the event and emulated many of the styles and motifs on display.

Although officially international, the Exhibition was dominated by the leading French craftsmen of the day, such as René Lalique – who designed for the event a 50-foot internally-lit glass fountain and waterfall – and master *ébéniste*, Jacques-Émile Ruhlmann, who designed the central pavilion, named the "Pavilion for a Rich Collector". Each of the major department stores, such as the Galleries Lafayette and Printemps, had their own specially designed Pavilion. Most of the exhibits, and the rooms that housed them, were exotic and relatively traditional. The public were not yet ready for the creations of such craftsmen as Mies van der Rohe, whose Modernist, minimalist design for one of the Pavilions caused such dismay among the Exhibition's organizers that they wished to build a 12-foot wall around it. Such avant-garde schemes, which many people today regard as the epitome of the Art Deco style, were not widely adopted until the 1930s.

The *S. S. Normandie* was launched in 1935. Once again, the top craftsmen of the day were called in to furnish the liner, which became the floating embodiment of the Art Deco style: lighting fixtures were designed by Marius-Ernest Sabino and René Lalique, who was also responsible for the wall panels and glass tableware; murals were by Jean Dunand, Jean Dupas and Paul Jouve; furniture was by Jules Leleu and Alavoine, among others; wrought-iron work was by Raymond Subes, and the ceramic tiles for the bathrooms were by Jean Mayadon. Other ocean liners were furnished in a similarly luxurious and "modern" style – for example, *L'Atlantique*.

FURNITURE

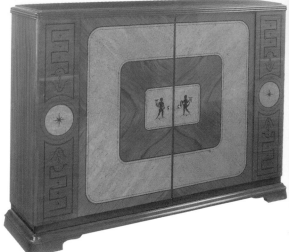

A Scandinavian mahogany and burrwood cabinet

Changing lifestyles after the First World War resulted in a demand for new types of furniture, such as elaborate dressing tables and cocktail cabinets. As luxury items, these were expected to be decorative as well as functional. Mass production was made possible by technological development, and many designers experimented with materials not previously used for furniture, such as tubular steel and glass. However, these innovations were carried out alongside the production of traditional types of furniture.

French pieces from the 1920s typify the more opulent style of Art Deco furniture. Designers such as J. E. Ruhlmann created expensive pieces for the nouveau riche elite. Forms were traditionalist, based on the late 18th and early 19thC Directoire period. Upholstery was luxuriant and well-sprung, incorporating colourful fabrics.

Wood veneers began to be replaced by polished and figured marble, and luxury woods, such as amboyna and macassar ebony, were also used. Late traditionalist work, such as that of Jules Leleu and Jean Dunand, makes extensive use of lacquered surfaces.

Süe et Mare exemplify the high watermark of Deco furniture. Their neo-traditionalist forms incorporate vibrant decorative motifs, often in ivory and mother-of-pearl, which elevate utilitarian furniture to the status of art objects. Rateau's furniture, also created for an elite market, is characterized by its use of metal, especially patinated bronze, employed on indoor furniture for the first time.

By 1925 this extravagant fashion had reached a peak: from then on traditional forms began to be supplanted by the Modernist creations advocated by Le Corbusier and the

Bauhaus. Even Ruhlmann eventually incorporated chromed tubular steel into his exotic macassar ebony veneered creations. Other innovative materials, such as plate glass, were promoted by René Lalique, who produced panels for furniture, and by master wrought iron workers such as Edgar Brandt. Formalized flowers gradually gave way to Cubist decoration, and other decorative elements, including those from Egyptian, Aztec and African art.

In contrast, very little British furniture from the 1930s is Modernist in style, with the notable exception of the cantilevered and streamlined forms of Jack Pritchard's Isokon (see p. 25). Among the most successful is that by Betty Joel, with its emphasis on form and wood grain. Utility is paramount; pieces have a sculptural, balanced quality. Most of the 1930s furniture available in Britain today is by less distinguished designers. Forms were simple, with an emphasis on the craftsmanship necessary to produce an unfussy design. Pale woods, such as sycamore and burr walnut, were popular, and the wood grain was often used as the main decorative element. Oak continued to be used, following traditional construction methods, especially by Robert Thompson ("Mouseman") (see p. 35).

The German Bauhaus, which included several important designers, among whom were Walter Gropius, Marcel Breuer, Mies van der Rohe and Marianne Brandt, constituted a gathering together of architects and industrial designers who aimed to apply functionalism and minimalism to their work, rather than approaching furniture design from an applied arts point of view. They experimented with new and unusual materials such as concrete, tubular steel and plate glass. Nothing escaped their influence or treatment; their design principles extended from buildings to the cutlery in a canteen. Any Bauhaus piece commands a premium. Most items carry monograms of individual designers; there is no Bauhaus mark. After the Nazis disbanded the organization on the grounds that it was subversive, many of its members, including Gropius and Mies van der Rohe, moved to the United States where their work was widely accepted.

American designers showed a preference for painted furniture: wood grain was seldom used as decoration; instead pieces were lacquered or painted in bold colours, often edged with primary colour or incorporating a silvered or gilt decorative element. When it is featured, wood grain is often contrasted with chrome. Pieces are large, as houses had interiors which could accommodate them; the skyscraper style was created to suit the smaller urban interiors which could not. The concern for functionalism was pioneered by Frank Lloyd Wright (see pp. 30-1).

Although many of the finest Deco furniture has remained in Paris, good-quality pieces do appear in some sales in Britain and the United States. Consult contemporary journals and periodicals such as *The Studio*: these offer the most useful illustrations, often never seen elsewhere.

JACQUES-EMILE RUHLMANN

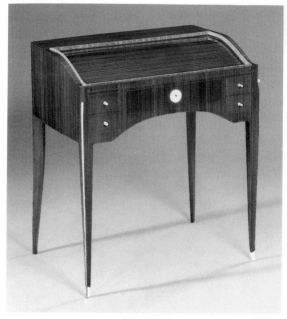

A lady's writing desk in macassar ebony and ivory by Ruhlmann c.1927; ht 35in/87cm; value code A

Identification checklist for Ruhlmann furniture
1. Does the piece exhibit signs of superior construction and craftsmanship?
2. Are the materials exotic and expensive?
3. Is the form simple, elegant and balanced?
4. Does the piece have discreet ivory embellishments – for example, stringing or chequering or perhaps a corner trim?
5. Is the decoration subtle?
6. If the item is small is it supported on tapering, slender legs, with ivory feet (possibly only at the front)?
7. If it is large, is it suspended above its base on pedestal supports with rectangular plinths?
8. Are all the joints of the construction completely covered, with surface joints used for decorative purposes only?
9. Is there a branded signature?

Recognition points
* On a number of Ruhlmann pieces the legs appear to emanate from outside the structure rather than supporting it from underneath.
* Drawered pieces are characterized by the smooth action and snug fit of the drawers.

Collecting

Ruhlmann's work is regarded as the best of the period. Although pieces turn up fairly regularly at auction, prices are among the highest of any paid for Art Deco furniture – as they were when they were made.

Marks

All Ruhlmann's work has a branded signature, "RUHLMANN", in letters $^1/_3$in (1cm) high, followed by the letter A, B or C, indicating from which of the three ateliers the piece emanated. A is considered the most desirable. After his death, his nephew, Alfred Porteneuve,

took over the workshops and repeated some of his designs, branded "PORTENEUVE" These are regarded as of lesser significance.
* Sometimes, only one piece from a suite bears a signature.

Woods

Macassar ebony was one of Ruhlmann's favourite exotic veneers, along with amboyna and shagreen. For contrast, he often combined these woods with ivory escutcheons and handles (as in the writing desk), or with decoration in mother-of-pearl or tortoiseshell.

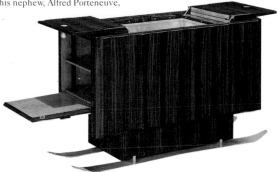

Many Ruhlmann pieces were made to individual commission, as was the highly unusual drinks cabinet on skis, *above*, from c.1930, which was also made in a lacquered version. Its characteristically heavy form is relieved by the use of wood grain for decorative effect.
* Ruhlmann furniture is hand-made. The joints are often carefully concealed – for example, any dovetailing on drawers, if visible at all, is very discreet.

Jacques-Emile Ruhlmann (French, 1879-1933)

Initially a painter, Ruhlmann became the best known French cabinet-maker of his day, following the tradition of the *ébénistes*. He designed for a rich and exclusive clientele, using exotic woods and other expensive materials. After the First World War he took over his father's successful building firm, Ruhlmann et Laurent, and expanded it with workshops devoted to furniture and other aspects of interior design.

As well as designing a wide range of furniture, including dining tables and chairs, beds, desks, secretaires, mirrors, upholstered armchairs and so on, Ruhlmann designed all manner of other items for interiors including textiles, light fixtures and even wastepaper baskets. Ruhlmann's

designs were mostly executed by craftsmen at his workshops, rather than by him personally.

Stylistic development

Many of Ruhlmann's most classic Art Deco pieces were in fact produced before 1920. Until the later part of the 1920s his work was in the traditionalist Art Deco style, based on simplified French Neo-classical designs and always in wood. After 1925 his designs became more cubist and less symmetrical, although always with a traditional concern for elegance and quality. He then began to incorporate some functional metal components, and later, during the 30s, made more widespread use of metal, tubular steel and plastic, although he never moved toward the functionalism of the Modernists.

PAUL FOLLOT

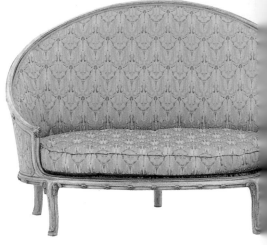

*A sofa and chair from a set of furniture designed by Paul Follot
c.1915-1920; ht of sofa 43¹/₂in/110cm; value code A*

Identification checklist for furniture designed by Paul
Follot
1. Has the piece been designed with a traditional
attention to comfort?
2. On upholstered furniture is the form relatively
restrained so that the upholstery becomes the main
decorative focus?
3. Does the piece exhibit a high level of craftsmanship in
construction and decoration?
4. On unupholstered pieces is the emphasis on form, as
much as, or more than on decoration?
5. Is the form balanced?
6. Is there any carved floral decoration (especially on
early pieces) or inlay work?
7. Do even the heavy pieces look relatively lightweight
and elegant?
8. Does the piece employ pale-coloured woods, possibly
lacquered or gilt?

___

Note
Collectors of Follot should try to familiarize themselves with the full
range of his furniture, as, perhaps more with Follot than any other
craftsman of the period, his pieces covered the entire style spectrum,
ranging from distinctly traditional, like the set *above*, to high Art Deco
as in the dressing table shown on the next page. In Follot's case a
checklist can provide only a very general guideline to his work.

Recognition point
A carved budding rose, known today as a "Follot rose", is often found
on Follot's work, especially on back rails and chair splats.

Paul Follot (French, 1877-1941)

Follot was a general interior designer, and as well as furniture designed textiles, wallpaper, ceramics and silverware.

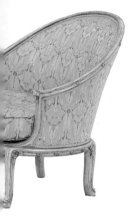

Early work

Follot's early work, produced before the mid-20s, was based on late 18thC forms, with an emphasis on comfort. Giltwood frames with bright upholstery, as used on the pieces in the main picture, were a common feature of his furniture in this period. He preferred to design complete interiors or sets of furniture, and this sofa and chair are part of a set that includes a chaise-longue, three armless chairs and a small table.

Designs tend to be restrained, with controlled embellishment and an emphasis on simple forms. The upholstery may provide the main decoration. Floral decoration became gradually more stylized as Follot's career progressed, and was later dispensed with in favour of inlaid decoration.

Collecting

The slightly less avant-garde designs are the most readily available. Pieces are seldom signed.

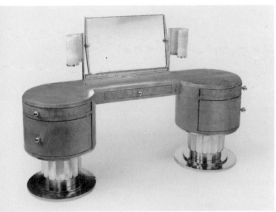

This dressing table from c.1925 represents the more Modernist end of the spectrum of Follot's work. Even so, it is made from lacquered wood, rather than one of the "new" materials such as amboyna or macassar ebony. Not all his Modernist works date from a later period – some from the pre-war era seem to anticipate the move toward more streamlined, innovative forms that occurred in the early 1930s. Although his designs became increasingly geometric or cubist, he never followed the route toward functionalism, and his furniture was clearly intended to be comfortable as well as attractive. *Follot eschewed modern materials, developing instead a growing interest in the possibilities of wood, particularly light woods. He began by experimenting with inlays, gilding, veneers and lacquer, and then became increasingly preoccupied with bringing out the contrasts between different woods.

15

SÜE ET MARE

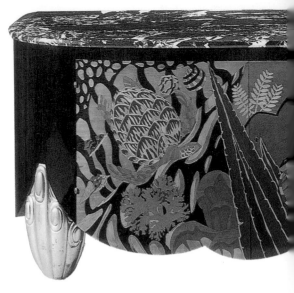

*A Süe et Mare macassar ebony marquetry giltwood and marble commode
c.1925; 33 x 68in/84.5 x 173cm; value code A*

Identification checklist for Süe et Mare furniture
1. Is the form essentially traditional, and perhaps
curvaceous?
2. Is the decoration elaborate, and typically French?
3. Is the quality of craftsmanship high – for example, are
any fixtures ormolu, and well-cast?
4. Does the piece make use of exotic veneers or
elaborate inlays, possibly combined with mother-of-
pearl?
5. Is it large with a solid appearance?
6. Are any feet relatively stylized or elaborately
decorated?

Identification point
Many Süe et Mare commodes and tables have marble tops.

Süe et Mare (French, 1919-28)
Louis Süe and André Mare, both
established French designers,
became partners to set up their
"Compagnie des Arts Français" in
1919. The company soon became
better known by their combined
surnames, and its work epitomizes
the opulence of French high Art
Deco style. It made a range of
furniture including chairs,
commodes and bureaux and also
designed coordinated interiors,
using a large team of prominent
16

designers, including Maurice
Marinot, Pierre Poisson and
André Vera. As well as wood
furniture, the company also
produced some in wrought-iron,
and a number of decorative
objects, including mirror frames,
chandeliers and table lamps, all
using stylized natural forms.
  Many Süe et Mare pieces were
commissioned rather than made
for mass production and as such
exhibit very high standards of
workmanship.

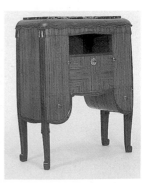

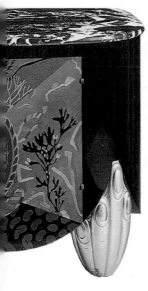

Although this fall-front bureau from c.1923 is not as elaborately embellished as the more typical piece shown on the opposite page, it nevertheless has several recognizably Sue et Mare features, including:
* marble slab top
* scrolled feet
* ormolu fittings
* curved elements in the construction
* the use of veneers to relieve a heavy form – in this case, contrasting pale and dark woods, and a delicate scalloped frieze around the top.

Marks
The furniture is unmarked: the style itself was considered a sufficient trademark.

Forms and styles
The company aimed to produce a purely French style, free from German influence. Many forms looked back to the era of Louis-Philippe, resulting in furniture that is both comfortable and luxurious, and often almost Baroque in its extravagance. Many Süe et Mare pieces are of massive proportions, with traditional forms relieved by intricate decoration, such as inlays, often in pale woods, depicting large floral bouquets or flower vase motifs, and sometimes incorporating mother-of-pearl. Some pieces also incorporate lacquer work. Follot-style roses sometimes also appear (see p. 14). Even the most traditional forms are given unusual touches which are superfluous to the structure – for example, while the piece in the main picture has an essentially traditional form, it has extraordinary, highly original stylized melon-like feet. On other furniture the feet often appear to be fixed to the outside of the body, rather than being an integral part of it.

Note
Süe et Mare's furniture often incorporated bronze and other metal embellishments by Maurice-Guiraud-Riviére and other leading metalworkers.

Later work
In 1928 the designer Jacques Adnet of the *Maison Fontaine* took over the direction of the company, but Süe continued his activities there as an artist and designer (and also returned to the practice of architecture). Under the leadership of Adnet the whole direction of its work changed, turning away from the sumptuous style toward Modernism and the increased use of metal.

Copies
A few lesser French companies copied the work of Süe et Mare. However, despite a superficial similarity there is little likelihood of mistaking the copy for the original, which is always of the highest quality – for example, copies of Süe et Mare's lacquered furniture are painted rather than ebonized or inlaid.

JEAN DUNAND

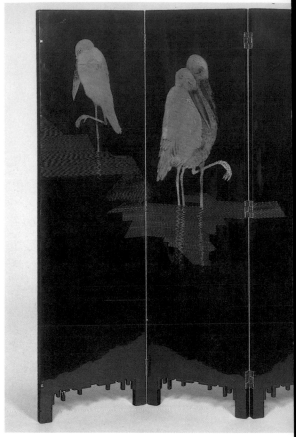

A lacquered wood four-panel screen by Jean Dunand
c.1930; ht 67in/168cm; value code A

Identification checklist for Jean Dunand furniture and metalwork

1. Is the decoration in metalwork – for example, patinated bronze, or silver inlay or, alternatively in very high-quality lacquer, possibly combined with eggshell?

2. Is the work richly made, with expensive materials and a high level of craftsmanship?

3. Is the surface highly polished?

4. Is there an element of Oriental or African influence in the colours or subject matter?

5. Is there an incised signature? (Bear in mind that not all Dunand's works are signed.)

6. Is the piece relatively simple in shape, but with lavish surface decoration?

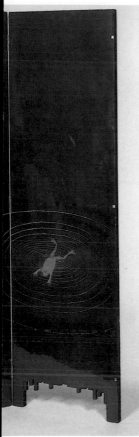

Jean Dunand (Swiss 1877-1942)

Dunand, who moved to Paris in 1896, was a prolific metalworker, lacquerist and furniture designer who produced expensive high-quality pieces for the most exclusive end of the market; all pieces were hand-made and many were specially commissioned. In 1912 he learned lacquerwork for which he became best known. His early work featured naturalistic designs, but in common with many craftsmen working throughout the first half of the 20thC, his style became progressively more geometric.

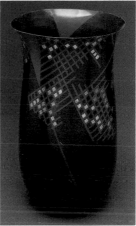

Dunand often worked in metal and was particularly interested in dinanderie – a technique of applying patinated enamelling over a non-precious metal, such as copper or steel. Like his screens, the vases often have sharp angular lines and a geometrical bias, evident in the lacquered dinanderie example *above*. Red and black was a favourite combination on vases, possibly reflecting the Oriental influence behind much of his work.

* Dunand often applied lacquerwork to his screens and panels. A Japanese influence is apparent on many pieces.

* Eggshell was often used on both inner and outer surfaces to give a textured effect.

Recognition point

Screens often have dentated lower edges, as in the example shown opposite.

Note

Dunand used many styles in his career, and his naturalistic work, which shows a close attention to realistic detail, is very different from his geometric designs, which are highly stylized. The questions in the checklist should therefore be regarded as general identification guidelines, and collectors should familiarize themselves with the full range of Dunand's work.

Marks

Not all Dunand's work is signed. However, some pieces are marked "JEAN DUNAND", sometimes with a serial number. Others have the words "JEAN DUNAND 72 RUE HALLE PARIS MADE IN FRANCE."

LUDWIG MIES VAN DER ROHE

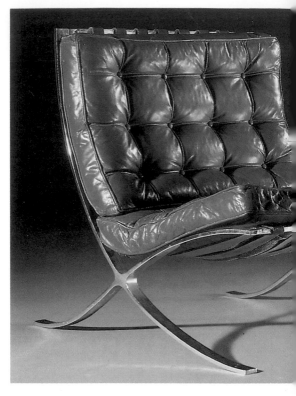

The Barcelona chair, designed by Mies van der Rohe, in tubular steel and leather
c.1931; ht 30in/75.5cm; value code A

Identification checklist for Mies van der Rohe furniture
1. Is the basic structure in chromed tubular steel combined with leather, raffia or glass?
2. Are the design and construction reduced to simple elements?
3. Does the form follow the function?
4. Does the piece have clarity and elegance of line?
5. In the case of a chair, is it cantilevered, possibly on X-stretchers, without feet?
6. Does any upholstery contribute visually to the structure as well as providing a degree of comfort?
7. Is the piece highly finished, with attention to detail?

Identification
All Mies van der Rohe's pieces were made by machine rather than by hand, and are not stamped. Many are still in production, although with minor changes to the basic designs. If in doubt, consult contemporary catalogues for detailed information on design and construction.

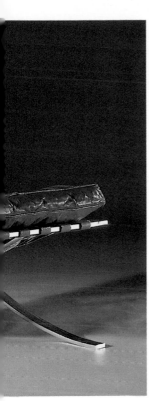

Ludwig Mies van der Rohe
(German, 1886-1969)

In both his glass skyscraper architecture and his furniture design, Mies van der Rohe is the doyen of the Modernist approach. He was one of the chief promoters of the Bauhaus machine-age philosophy. In 1938 he emigrated to the United States and in 1944 became an American citizen.

From 1927 to 1931 his furniture was produced by the small firm of Berliner Metallgewerbe Joseph Muller. Thereafter it was made by Bamberger Metalwerkstätten, and marketing was handled by Thonet-Mundus.

In his furniture designs Mies van der Rohe combines classical forms with Modernism. He achieves a machine-made look but with careful hand-finishing and close attention to detail.

Collecting

Original furniture dating back to Mies van der Rohe's time at the Bauhaus, and before mass-production began, fetches very high prices – as much as ten times that of the later models – particularly in the case of classics such as the Barcelona chair.

The Barcelona chair

The Barcelona chair, *above*, was first exhibited in 1929, and is one of the most popular of all 20thC chair designs. It was not mass-produced until after the Second World War but has been in continuous production since (recently by Knoll Associates).

The chairs are not stamped but one way for a collector to distinguish between the early examples and later mass-produced models is from the construction: the top rail of the original version, shown here, was in bent chromed flat steel, with separate sections joined by lap joints and screwed with chrome-headed bolts. Leather straps were used for additional support and also made the chair more comfortable. In later versions the top rail is in cut and welded stainless steel. Most of the chairs retain their original upholstery.

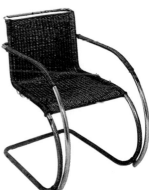

Mies van der Rohe's famous cantilevered tubular designs first went into production in 1927, the date of this armchair, *above*, which is made of chrome-plated steel tubes. The leather seat is laced on the underside and the back is held in place with a metal strip and screws. Similar versions exist but without arms. Also in this range of cantilevered tubular furniture were steel coffee tables and stools with a leather sling top.

21

MARCEL BREUER

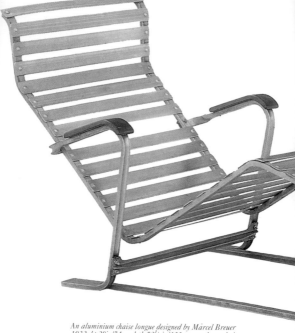

*An aluminium chaise longue designed by Marcel Breuer
1932; ht 29in/74cm, lgth 52¹/₂in/133 cm.; value code A*

Identification checklist for Breuer furniture
1. Does the piece contain tubular steel, laminated wood or aluminium?
2. Does the form follow the function?
3. Are the contours simple?
4. Does the piece make any concessions to comfort, perhaps through a careful balance between a soft seat and a hard frame?
5. If the piece is metal, is it light in look and weight, perhaps with an additional transparent quality?
6. If an upright chair, does the seat appear to float, suspended between the structural elements?
7. Does the piece have only minimal decoration, if any?
8. Does it contain any geometric elements?
9. Are there any cantilevered elements (after 1923)?

Recognition point
Runners, instead of feet, were used increasingly on chairs and tables after 1925, and contribute to the impression that Breuer's tubular steel furniture was made in one piece.

Reproductions
Modern reproductions exist. However, these lack the characteristic signs of wear of the original pieces.

Marcel Lajos Breuer
(Hungarian, 1902-81)

Breuer moved from Hungary to the Bauhaus in Weimar in 1920. Some of his designs were manufactured in England by PEL and by Thonet in Austria from 1928. He worked briefly for Isokon in England in 1936 (see p. 25). In 1937 he joined his ex-colleague Walter Gropius in America. His laminated furniture shares design affinities with that of the Finnish designer, Aalvar Aalto.

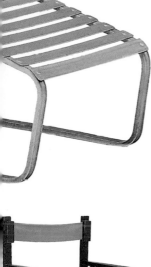

Breuer made several versions of this 1922 oak chair. The design may have been inspired by Rietveld's famous 1919 chair. The floating impression of the seat, and the apparently unsupported arms are typical. A degree of comfort has been sacrificed for the sake of the functionalist form.

Materials and styles

Breuer revolutionized utility furniture, promoting the use of tubular steel, plywood and aluminium. He made desks, cabinets, tables, and folding or stacking pieces and designed furniture for specific interiors.

From the early 1920s Breuer experimented with plywood. With its cantilevered construction and simple vertical and horizontal planes, the armchair shown bottom left is typical of much of his furniture of the period.

By c.1925, inspired by the construction of his new bicycle, Breuer recognized the potential of tubular steel in furniture. Writing of his new enthusiasm, he declared: "metal furniture is part of a modern room. It is 'styleless', for it is not expected to express any particular styling beyond its purpose and the construction necessary thereof." Another departure from tradition was his use of hide for upholstery, rather than canvas.

Initially quite rough, the steel gradually became more refined over the years and, though thinner, was stronger. This meant that designs were continually "updated" in response to technological changes. Thus collectors should expect small variations between furniture made in different years, even if the basic design is the same.

In 1932 Breuer produced his first aluminium furniture. It had a silvery finish which could be left dull or shiny. Designs tended to have more curves than the tubular steel furniture because the aluminium was lighter and required more support.

In 1936 Breuer adapted some of his earlier designs to plywood – for example, the chaise longue, which became the Isokon "short chair". For Isokon he also produced some innovative nesting tables and stools which provided the inspiration for much of the furniture of the 40s.

Attribution

Breuer's work is not signed or stamped, although Thonet and DIM, for whom he made many designs, have makers' labels. Attribution can be ascertained by consulting contemporary catalogues. There are also catalogues for PEL and Standard-Mobel, who produced some of his tubular steel chairs.

FINMAR

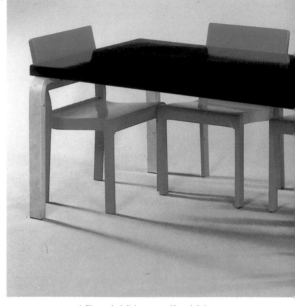

A Finmar Ltd dining room table and chairs
table: 1933-5; ht 28in/71cm; chairs: 1929; ht 31in/79cm; value code D

Identification checklist for Finmar furniture
1. Is the piece plywood?
2. Is the form very plain and simple, with no surface decoration?
3. Does the piece have a metal label?
4. Do chairs or side tables stack?
5. Is the piece solid looking?
6. Are the colours bold and striking and perhaps limited to only one or two, used in solid blocks?

Finmar (British, 1934/5-1939)
Finmar Ltd was established in 1934/5 as the British importers and distributors of furniture designed and produced by Aalvar Alto, a Finnish architect and designer. The first stacking furniture was made in 1927. From 1929 Aalto began to use plywood in his furniture, especially to make chairs and tea trolleys. The stacking stools designed by Aalto and produced by Korhonen in Turko between 1930 and 1933 were very popular, largely because they were eminently versatile and practical. In 1935 he established his firm Artek to produce his

furniture designs, door furniture and lighting.

Marks
Some of the furniture made by Aalto in Finland is marked "Aalto Mobler, Svensk Kvalitet Sprodurt". Finmar pieces are not signed. The *Decorative Arts Journal* shows the full range of their wares. Most items carry an applied metal label bearing the model number. Some sets – for example, of dining furniture – may have been made at different dates: the chairs of the set shown above were designed 4-6 years before the table.

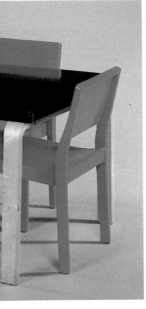

ISOKON (British, 1932-39)

Plywood furniture was also made by Isokon. Jack Pritchard, who founded the firm, had been designing furniture since the end of the 1920s, but Isokon (from "Isometric Unit Construction") was not set up to produce the designs in quantity until 1932. In 1936 the firm was renamed Isokon Furniture Company and Walter Gropius became Controller of Design he emigrated to America in the following year. Marcel Breuer was the leading designer, particularly remembered for his "long chair" (see p. 22). The firm closed at the outbreak of war but was reopened in 1963.

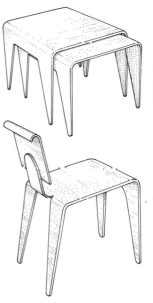

Styles and construction

Most Finmar furniture has a multiple construction element (unlike say, items made by Isokon, which are often from a single piece of plywood: see right). A striking impact is achieved through use of bold blocks of strong strident colours, rather than through surface decoration, which is usually absent. Most pieces, especially those required to bend, were made from plywood (although table tops are of solid wood), and are Modernist in every sense, with clean contours and no concessions to decoration. The pieces in the range were designed to complement and harmonize with one another both stylistically and practically – thus proportions are such that sets can be made using many different combinations of chairs, tables and so on.

* Laminated plywood tends to chip and flake, and furniture in this medium has not survived in quantity.
* Chairs and *chaises longues* were designed to accept loose-fitting padded cushions. Examples that retain their original cushions command a premium.

Isokon attempted to produce more adventurous forms than those of Finmar. Most pieces were in plywood and some were built-in. The firm is mostly remembered for its "cut-out" furniture – pieces, especially side chairs and tables such as those illustrated, *above* – were cut and moulded from a single sheet of plywood, and were lightweight and easily assembled. They were originally manufactured in Estonia by Venesta. There were several versions of the chairs and tables, including a dining table version.

25

PAUL FRANKL

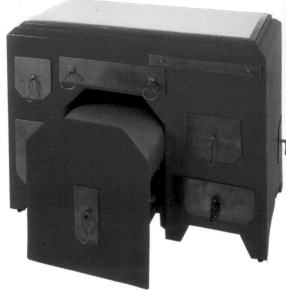

A red lacquered "puzzle" desk by Paul Frankl
c.1927; ht 33in/84cm; value range A-B

Identification checklist for Frankl furniture
1. Is the piece elegant in style, showing a strong architectural influence?
2. Is the surface lacquered, with metal or bakelite inlays or fittings?
3. Is there very little surface decoration?
4. Does the piece have a named metal tag?
5. Is any trim red and black in colour with a turquoise, blue or green interior?
6. Does it use pale-coloured American woods, such as birch or maple?

Paul T. Frankl (The United States, 1886-1958)
Frankl was born in Austria and emigrated to the United States during the First World War. He was one of the USA's pioneer Modernists and the first furniture designer to reflect contemporary architecture, a result of his early training in architecture and engineering. In the late 1920s he wrote five books and a number of influential articles on form and design. Frankl's early work, from before 1920, is relatively undistinguished and European in style, in accordance with the

tastes of his fashionable American clientele. Later work, from 1925 onwards, is more individual and thus collectable.

There is an element of novelty about all Frankl pieces, seen in the "puzzle desk", *above*, from 1927, so named because of its concealed seat and the asymmetrical placement of its drawers. Frankl's designs place an emphasis on geometry, and their sometimes severe outlines are almost Neo-Biedermeier in style.
* Frankl furniture from the early 1920s favours oak and metal, often with ebonized frames.

26

Skyscraper furniture

Frankl is perhaps best known for his range of Skyscraper furniture. This style, which he pioneered in 1925 and continued working in until 1930, showed an awareness of the needs of smaller, urban spaces. The name evokes New York's remarkable Art Deco architecture, and was used by Frankl as a trade mark.

Many of the pieces are multi-functional and combine cupboards, display units and bookcases. They are frequently made of California redwood, usually with a red, silver or black lacquered trim; interiors are in turquoise, blue or green, and may have plastic or metallic finishes.

* Check the condition of lacquering and metallic paint, which are easily marked or scratched, as on the arms, for example, of the chair shown *right*. A small degree of wear is to be expected, and is acceptable provided the decoration has not worn away completely.

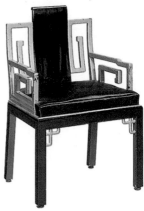

This "Chinese" chair from around 1930, with its contrasted red and black lacquering and gold detailing, reflects Frankl's interest in the Orient and Oriental styles, following a trip to the Far East early in the 1920s. Sets are hard to come by. Furniture of this type complemented the highly popular Chinese style of 1930s interior design.

* Like the Skyscraper pieces, Frankl's other furniture from the late 1920s is in wood with brightly coloured lacquered and painted surfaces. In this period he exploited the potential of mirrored glass, often using it for tops of pieces, together with bakelite and metal fittings, giving an almost theatrical effect. Pieces from this period are usually innovative in style, like the bookcase unit shown, *left*, and highly collectable.

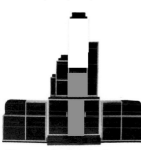

Skyscraper furniture is often simple in appearance, with pure uncluttered lines. This lacquered and silvered wood bookcase unit from 1928 is typical in its rectilinear, pyramidal form, scant decoration and simple construction.

* The standard of cabinetry on Skyscraper pieces is usually poor. They have not been commercially reproduced, but modern copies do exist.

* Other American designers, such as Kem Weber, Abel Faidy Norman Bel Geddes and J. B. Peters, also adopted the Skyscraper form, in other media as well as furniture. Their work is less collectable, so check that pieces bear the Frankl mark – a metal tag, stamped "Skyscraper Furniture, Frankl Galleries, 4 East 48th Street, New York".

Later work

After 1930 Frankl turned his back on the Skyscraper furniture concept and concentrated instead on metal furnishings, producing tubular chromed chairs and consoles and Formica-topped metal tables. In keeping with the ideas of the period, these meet with strict standards of functionalism, and can be compared with the work of Donald Deskey (see pp. 28-9).

* In the 1930s Frankl also produced an innovative range of sun parlour and patio seat furniture in wicker and other cane fibres, reviving a popular Victorian style but adding angular corners and armrests in keeping with the spirit of Modernism.

27

DONALD DESKEY

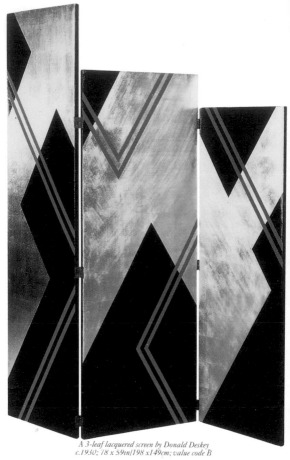

A 3-leaf lacquered screen by Donald Deskey
c.1930; 78 x 59in/198 x149cm; value code B

Identification checklist for the furniture and lights of
Donald Deskey

1. Are the forms based on rectilinear lines and geometry,
with a complete absence of ornament?

2. If furniture, does the item incorporate a metal or
metallic surface contrasted with a bold primary colour?

3. Is there any evidence of the designer's attention to
simplicity and economy of construction?

4. Does the item have the appearance of an "industrial
prototype"?

5. Are any of the materials extremely unusual and
possibly unprecedented?

6. Does the item show a particularly high standard of
construction?

Donald Deskey (American, 1894-1989)

By the late 1920s Deskey, who began his career in an advertising agency, had achieved recognition as a furniture and product designer. He combined a taste for functionalism with a uniquely American flair and mastery of the "streamlined" style. His work for private commissions was of unique design and rarely appears on the market today.

Deskey-Vollmer

Most Deskey pieces found today were produced between 1927 and 1931 with Deskey's business partner Phillip Vollmer. These were designed to be economically manufactured on an industrial scale, although many were ultimately produced in small quantities. Tables, seating, small desks, chests and a range of innovative lighting devices were made in brushed or chromium-plated steel in bent form, tubular steel and plate glass, often coloured, which gave them a "Bauhaus" look. Aluminium, bakelite and cork were also used.

Commissioned products

In the late 1920s Deskey worked in collaboration with Frankl (see pp. 26-7), and on commission for several American manufacturers, including Eskey, Amodec and the firm of Schmeig, Hungate and Kotzian (all New York-based firms). Most of this was wood-veneered furniture of more conventional design than the Deskey-Vollmer products, and tends to be less collectable today. Finishes include macassar ebony, sometimes in combination with brass, and a variety of blond woods, as well as some painted surfaces. Commissioned work also included designs for entire interiors

Marks

Much Deskey furniture is unsigned, although most designs are recorded in modern publications. Small items and lighting are rarely signed, but some furniture bears Deskey-Vollmer tags, and other manufacturers used their own stamps or tags, although these do not always credit Deskey as the designer.

EUGENE SCHOEN (American, 1880-1957)

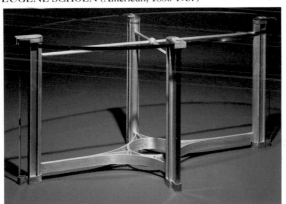

Another important American craftsman, Schoen, initially an architect, was designing furniture, fabrics and rugs by 1920. He was particularly influenced by the style and principles of the Wiener Werkstätte (see pp. 158-9), although much of his furniture is characterized by the use of luxurious materials including exotic woods, often edged in silver leaf, with silk or calf skin upholstery. Products were small-scale and extremely elegant, showing traces of Neo-classical or Biedermeier influence. By the late 1920s and early 30s, he was also working in the more familiar materials of modern American taste, exemplified by this glass and nickel table. His furniture was retailed by Eugene Schoen Inc., and may bear the name of the maker Schmeig, Hungate and Kotzian. Most items are made to high standards of craftsmanship and many are unique.

FRANK LLOYD WRIGHT

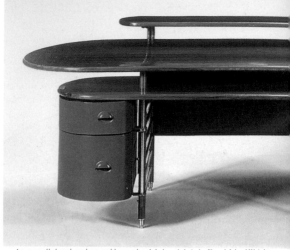

An enamelled steel, walnut and brass-plated desk and chair by Frank Lloyd Wright c.1937; ht 33in/85cm; value code A

Identification checklist for Frank Lloyd Wright furniture
1. Is the form imaginative, with an architectural influence?
2. Are the decorative elements incorporated into the form, rather than being added to the surface?
3. Is the design based on bold, geometric shapes and parallel lines and curves?
4. Is the use of any colour dramatic, perhaps depending on just one or two colours applied in simple, solid blocks for maximum impact?
5. Is the piece devoid of fussy details?
6. If it is all wood, does it have a solid, chunky appearance?
7. If the piece is a chair, is it comparatively high-backed?
8. Does it sacrifice a degree of comfort for visual appeal?

Collecting Frank Lloyd Wright
As Frank Lloyd Wright is one of the most famous architect/designers of this century, his work commands high prices, especially as many pieces were made to private commission, rather than mass-produced. Unique designs and those made as one of a very limited series inevitably command a premium. The furniture is unsigned, but the provenance of individual pieces is usually well-documented. Wright worked in a range of media: he designed copper urns and other decorative metalwares, table lamps, textiles and ceramics, notably tablewares for the Japanese/American firm Noritake (see pp. 96-7). His architectural plates and drawings are also highly collectable. His work is more readily available in the United States than elsewhere.

Fakes
Wright's furniture is not known to have been faked, although there are some honest reproductions, which, unlike the originals, do not have signs of wear and tear.

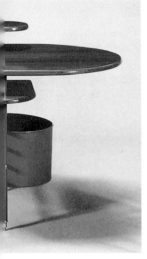

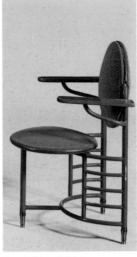

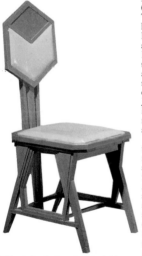

**Frank Lloyd Wright
(American, 1867-1959)**
The foremost exponent of the
Prairie School, an American
Modernist movement in domestic
architecture established c.1895,
Frank Lloyd Wright's furniture
shows an unmistakeably
architectural influence; indeed,
some pieces, such as the desk and
chair above, made for the S. C.
Johnson Administration building
in Wisconsin, were designed to
reflect the interior and exterior
architecture of a building.

Wright designed furniture from
the end of the 19thC until the
middle of the 20thC, but pieces
are usually fairly easy to date:
furniture of the 1920s retains an
Arts and Crafts/Art Nouveau feel,
although the form is almost
always innovative. Most pieces
are in wood, usually oak, and
often hand-made. Shapes and
motifs are commonly cubistic or
angular, many reflecting a Mayan,
Aztec or Japanese influence.

During the 1930s, designs
become progressively more
functional and utilitarian, with
decoration kept to a minimum,
usually as an integral part of the
form.

By the late 1930s pieces were
machine-produced partly or
wholly in metal, and designs were
becoming progressively more
adventurous. Wright returned to
wood in the 1950s.

This chair, designed c.1916-22,
has several features typical of
Wright's work in these years:
* the use of oak
* a functionalist form
* the Japanese influence – for
example, the dramatic use of
zigzags, and the absence of
surface decoration
* the use of upholstery (in this
case, a yellow oil cloth) to soften
a hard form.

31

BETTY JOEL

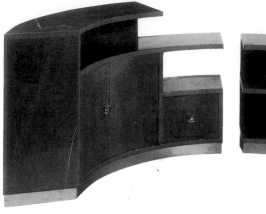

A pair of Betty Joel satinwood display cabinets
c.1930; ht 27½in/70cm, wdth 54in/137.5cm; value code C

Identification checklist for Betty Joel furniture
1. Is the piece imposing and solid-looking?
2. Are the contours gentle and curved?
3. Is the piece devoid of carving or surface decoration?
4. Is a decorative feature made of the wood grain?
5. Is the piece labelled?
6. Are any fixtures simple and unfussy?
7. Is the piece hand-finished?

Betty Joel (English, 1896-1984)

Betty Joel was born in China. In 1921 she established a furniture workshop in Hayling Island, followed by a factory in Portsmouth, a shop in London, and another factory in Kingston. Much of her work was commissioned – for example, designs for film sets and some exclusive dwellings. Many pieces, especially bedroom furniture and wall cabinets, are built-in. Joel's furniture is large in size, as it was intended for the spacious rooms of London mansion flats. It is usually highly practical, and even versatile, such as the pair of cabinets above. She also designed rugs, produced in China, and textiles, produced in France.
* Betty Joel designed some unit furniture for the Gordon Russell company (see pp. 34-5) in 1934.

Decoration

Designs from the early 1920s are often heavily upholstered and paired with signed rugs (see p. 175). By the end of the 1920s Joel had developed a more distinctive furniture style, and her 1930s pieces are simpler and more geometric.

Joel furniture is simple and unfussy, and usually devoid of carved decoration and painted finishes. Some pieces are lacquered, but Joel had a strong preference for featuring the wood grain as the main, or sole decorative element. Alternatively, a decorative effect is sometimes achieved through the use of contrasting veneers.

Construction

All pieces are hand-finished, although some machinery was used in the construction. The quality of the craftsmanship is excellent – for example, drawers are likely to fit very snugly, so that air rushes out when they are closed.

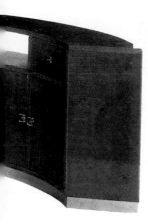

HEAL & SON (1810-present)

Ambrose Heal (1872-1959) designed all the furniture for the family firm from 1896 until the 1950s. Like the work of Betty Joel, his early pieces have a strong affinity with the English Arts and Crafts Movement.

Furniture has an architectural look, with the wood grain as the chief decorative element. Heals preferred light-coloured woods, especially limed oak. After the First World War they began to use weathered oak instead of unpolished wood. Work of the 1930s is more avant garde, although not to the same degree as French furniture, and tends to combine contemporary features with more traditional elements.

Furniture is hand-finished, but is made using modern techniques such as screw-fixing. Most pieces are stamped or labelled.

Materials

Joel avoided the luxury woods, such as macassar ebony, that were popular at the time, preferring conservatively grained woods, arranged to achieve an almost monochromatic effect. Her furniture from the 1930s makes use of industrially produced plywood laminates and other man-made materials. The use of chromed steel for the plinths of this display cabinet is quite innovative.

Form

Form is given priority over decoration, and pieces are strong and solid-looking. Some use is made of geometric and angular shapes, but Joel favoured ellipses and curved contours – such as those in this satinwood display cabinet – which she described as "silhouettes of the female form". Dressing tables often incorporate large circular mirrors.

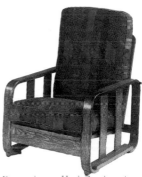

Decoration on Heals furniture is usually kept to a minimum and is very simple, as in the sides of the chair *above*.

Handles and drawers

Handles are simple, usually of a grip rather than a hanging type. Drawer edges may be cross-banded, as they are on this example.

Marks

Furniture bears a glazed paper label affixed to the reverse of the piece, which gives the date and signature of the designer and craftsman, and usually also reads "Made at the Token Works, Kingston." (The name Token was derived from a combination of the words teak and oak.)

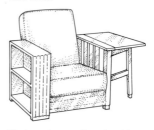

Heals made a number of multiple utility items. The example *above* is typical, combining a chair consisting of two upholstered pads, with a side table and bookcase. Examples with original fabric can still be found today.

33

GORDON RUSSELL

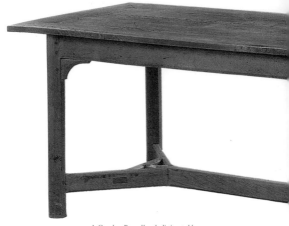

A Gordon Russell oak dining table
1923; ht 30in/76cm, lgth 66in/168cm; value code D

Identification checklist for Russell furniture
1. Is the piece hand-made with a hand-finished surface?
2. Is the form relatively plain, with an emphasis on careful construction rather than on carving and surface decoration?
3. Is the piece strong and solidly constructed, with all the elements contributing to the structure, including those that also have a decorative value?
4. Is it all wood, with dowel joints and no metal?
5. Are the pegs and other elements of the structure clearly visible?

Gordon Russell (British, 1892-1980)
A member of the Cotswold School of the early 20thC, Russell advocated the use of traditional construction techniques and never really made the transition to the Modernist materials and styles adopted in Continental Europe during the 1920s and 30s. He made a wide range of items, including dining room, bedroom and office furniture.

Russell was primarily a designer; it is unlikely that he made many pieces himself. Some furniture comes with a paper label; that of the table, *above*, is particularly detailed and reads: "This piece is a dining table in English quartered oak was designed by Gordon Russell and constructed by hand by G. Cooke in the workshop of Gordon Russell and Sons Broadway Worcestershire England
34

in May 1923." The workshop established by Russell is still in operation today.

Forms and decoration
Pieces are all hand-made, often in oak, with an emphasis on quality of construction. No use is made of carving or other decoration, as the form was considered sufficient in itself. Even those concessions to ornament, such as the ear pieces (the shaped sections between the legs and the frieze) and the spandrels in the corners of this table, are primarily functional and only incidentally decorative. The stretcher, of a type known as a double hayrake stretcher, is an innovative element in an otherwise conventional form, but also makes an important structural contribution as it provides added strength. The peg construction used is clearly visible.

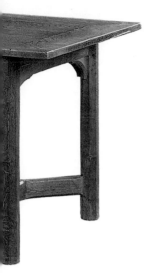

PETER WAALS (English, dates unknown)

Another member of the Cotswold School, Waals designed furniture that was quintessentially British. Like that of Russell, his work looks back more to Arts and Crafts and Art Nouveau than forward to Art Deco, although its functional appearance gives it something in common with the Modernist furniture produced elsewhere in Europe. He preferred country woods, especially walnut, cedar, oak and limed oak. Pieces are rarely signed, but many are commissioned and so have an available history.

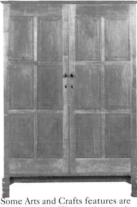

Some Arts and Crafts features are evident in this Waals walnut and cedar wardrobe from 1928 – for example, the use of the wood grain as a decorative element, and the stout, masculine, heavy form, which borders on the utilitarian. Typically, ornament is absent.

Condition

Ear pieces are vulnerable to being knocked and damaged. Make sure that they are original by checking that the wood corresponds in colour to the main piece. Collectors should expect to find some wear – for example, scratches or knocks on the feet and lower legs: this is not detrimental to value unless the damage is severe. Chairs are sometimes reupholstered so it is particularly important to check those with modern springing or modern-looking hide covers for signs of age, as the whole piece may be recent.

ROBERT THOMPSON, "Mouseman" (British, d.1955)

Thompson also followed the principles adopted by the Cotswold School. His work is largely undecorated, except for panelling and the occasional use of wrought-iron fixtures. The carved figure of a mouse, usually in relief but sometimes carved into a niche, became his trademark. Pieces are all in oak, and are given a sculpted, hand-made look by use of an adze. Mouseman furniture is still made today, but modern examples usually have a smooth finish. Commissions from the 1930s tend to be the most sought-after

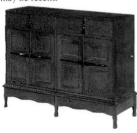

This fine Russell sideboard makes only a few concessions to ornament: carved laburnum handles, a moulded frieze and a waved apron. It has a solid, conservative appearance.

35

MINOR FURNITURE

Furniture of the 1920s and 30s is for the most part prohibitively expensive – as it was when first made. This is particularly true of work attributed to the top craftsmen. However, some good-quality furniture, much of it made in emulation of the most popular pieces of the period, is still affordable. Not all of it is worth buying: some pieces, especially those made in England, are rather large and clumsy and generally of poor quality. The most successful designs tend to be those of relatively plain form and simple lines, perhaps with the innovative elements combined with attractive supports or clever use of materials. Condition is also a factor. Some furniture of lesser quality may not have fared well – for example, leather upholstery can crack and veneers may deteriorate (although restoration is sometimes possible). The best of the less expensive furniture includes bedroom suites, which may comprise a wardrobe, dressing table and stool, and dining room tables and chairs, along with occasional tables. Light woods command a premium.

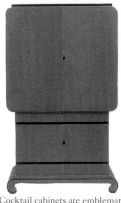

Cocktail cabinets are emblematic of the jazz age. This one is good quality although not of the most striking design. Many cocktail cabinets open to show an illuminated interior, the action of the door raising internal fixtures containing glasses and accessories.
* Biedermeier elements, such as the use of pale woods and an unornamanted design, often feature in Art Deco furniture, sometimes to dramatic effect.

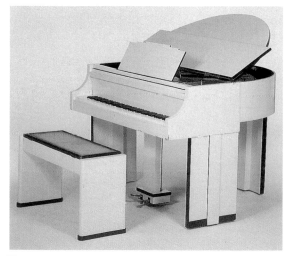

Pianos from the 1920s and 30s represent excellent value, especially if they are still in working order (although they nearly always need restringing). This 1930s grand is typical in its use of painted and lacquered effects rather than wood grain as the main decorative feature. The slab supports contribute to its overall avant-garde impression.
* The baby grands produced by Eavestaff are of a more saleable size.

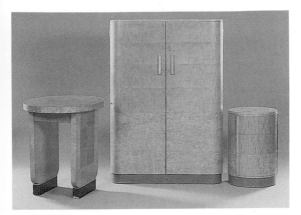

This is a modest but fairly attractive set of bedroom furniture in a desirable pale wood. It has several typical features:
* the use of wood grain as decoration
* plinths in a contrasting tone
* geometric forms.
Interiors are usually well fitted. Missing fitments should be reflected in the price. Veneers should also be intact.

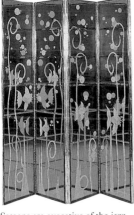

Screens are evocative of the jazz age, but even the best of them have never commanded high prices – perhaps because they are not very practical. A number were made in mirrored glass, which was also used for mirror frames and some small occasional tables. In England some rather sombre screens incorporating marquetry and stained wood landscapes were made by Rowley. This screen by an anonymous designer, in electric blue with exotic fish, is a particularly attractive example and has survived in good condition.

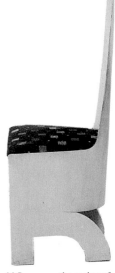

Gerald Summers, the maker of this laminated birchwood chair, was one of the few British designers to use innovative forms. He is particularly known for the seating he produced under commission for several British stores. His work is currently affordable, but may well become more expensive within the next few years.

GLASS

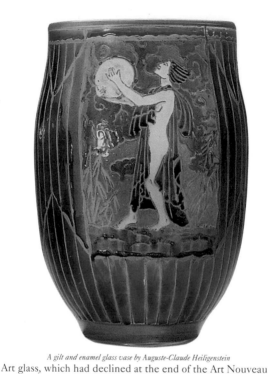

A gilt and enamel glass vase by Auguste-Claude Heiligenstein

Art glass, which had declined at the end of the Art Nouveau era, enjoyed a revival in the 1920s and 30s. During this period artists developed an awareness of the creative potential offered by glass, which was used in a variety of new ways, as a structural as well as a decorative medium. Architects and designers worked imaginatively with plate and mirror glass, and old techniques were adapted to suit new styles. Many of the more ornate items are apparently functional – for example, vases, bowls, and so on – but were intended to be primarily decorative.

The French were the leading innovative glassmakers of the time. Many well-designed pieces were also produced in the United States. British manufacturers produced a large quantity of pseudo-Georgian and pseudo-Victorian glassware alongside more modern articles.

Moulded glass is the most prolific area, and quality varies considerably. The leading artist in this field was René Lalique, whose wares were emulated by a number of other glassmakers, including Marius Ernest Sabino, and the firms of Verlys, Barolac, Etling and Valton, all of whom worked in moulded opalescent glass.

The best enamelled glass is by the French artists Marcel Goupy, Jean Luce, the firms of Baccarat, Decuper-Delvaux and Verdar, the Austrian designer Auguste-Claude Heiligenstein, and the Czech factories working in imitation of Baccarat. Enamelled glass is not as common as moulded glass, and usually commands a higher price.

Engraved glass was made primarily by the Swedish firm Orrefors and the American Steuben Glass Works. Major French designers working in the medium were Daum, and Maurice Marinot, who was emulated by Charles Schneider, Henri Navarre and André Thuret. In England engraved glass was produced by Thomas Webb after designs by W. Clyne Farquharson and Keith Murray.

The labour-intensive techniques of pâte de verre (glass paste heated until it fuses within the mould) and pâte de cristal (a similar process which achieves a near-transparent effect) were used to produce luxury items. The best pieces are by Gabriel Argy-Rousseau, Françoise-Emile Décorchement, Alméric Walter and Frederick Carder.

As with furniture, the demand for new forms arose from changes in lifestyle. For example, cocktail parties became the vogue once drinking had become a more socially acceptable pastime. The survival rate of cocktail glasses is poor. Products that became popular during this period include perfume bottles and car mascots, which both provide fruitful areas for collectors.

René Lalique dominated the market, and his vases, tablewares and car mascots are widely available. He also used glass for light fixtures and in architectural settings. There are many pseudo-Lalique light fixtures on the market: these are of obviously poorer quality, which is reflected in the prices.

There is a type of glass mass-produced during the 1930s in Europe and the United States referred to by the American term "Depression glass", which is angular and frosted in appearance, usually in murky colours, including muted green, peach or black; it is of simple moulded form. Depression glass consists largely of low-budget domestic wares, including shallow glass bowls with figural decoration, and figurines of tropical fish. It has little artistic or constructional merit, and seems unlikely ever to become highly collectable. Recently, cloud glass by the Gateshead firm of Davidson has become popular with collectors. This is often dark brown with a random swirling effect.

It is still possible to buy Deco glassware at a reasonable price. Decorative vases and bibelots – for example, small glass animals, are the objects most commonly found today. Few glasses have survived: many of those which have are enamelled, often with designs showing cockerels. Enamel wares by Delvaux have not yet acquired a status that makes them prohibitively expensive, and the market for perfume bottles, apart from the work of Lalique, is still very much in its infancy. Baccarat wares are still relatively underrated. There is also some good Czech glass available, especially the figural types and pieces with hand-engraving or geometric enamelling.

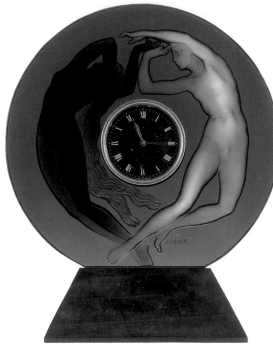

A René Lalique glass clock entitled Night and Day
c.1930; ht 14³/₄in/37.5cm; value code A

Identification checklist for Lalique glass
1. Is the piece marked?
2. Is the form inventive?
3. Are the form and decoration harmoniously balanced?
4. Is the style highly individual, and perhaps reminiscent of Art Nouveau, especially in figural work?
5. Is figural work detailed, with precisely rendered facial expressions?
6. If an animal, is it a bird, a fish or a horse?
7. Does clear glass have a dark tone compared with modern crystal?
8. Are any figures nude or semi-naked?
9. Is the glass opalescent?

René Lalique (French, 1860-1945)
Lalique, the foremost jeweller of the Art Nouveau period, became the leading glass designer of the Art Deco period, making a wide range of objects, including car mascots, perfume bottles, vases, tablewares and plates, clocks,

jewelry, lighting and figurines. Some of his glass was incorporated into furniture. Most wares were machine-made for the mass-market, although the perfume bottles were relatively expensive in their day as they often carried scent by top parfumiers.

The 1932 catalogue

The 1932 cataloogue of Lalique's wares (since reprinted) is essential to serious collectors as it carries almost the full range of items designed by Lalique, and the dates when they were first made. The catalogue also gives dimensions, but quoted heights should not be regarded as definitive, as proportions do vary slightly between pieces.

Alterations

Some pieces have been altered: vases may have had their handles removed whilst some shell bowls were converted to ceiling bowls, often with non-Lalique glass frosted surrounds, by the Brèves Gallery, who retailed most of the Lalique glass sold in England. Although these are quite obviously not Lalique factory productions, collectors in any doubt should check with the 1932 catalogue.

Opalescent glass

Most wares are opalescent, produced by adding phosphates, fluorine and aluminium oxide to the glass to make it opaque, and by adding a minute amount of cobalt to give an internal blue tint. High-relief areas are more opaque than thin-walled parts. (This technique was used by other glassmakers, notably Sabino – see pp. 54-5.) Opalescent glass was made only during Lalique's lifetime: most of the modern reproductions are in frosted or clear glass.

Condition

Unless the item is exceptionally rare, Lalique pieces must be in pristine condition to be of any great value. Chips can often be removed by grinding and polishing. Scrutinize the overall proportions of the piece as these are sometimes distorted – for example, in smoothing out chipped areas. The bases and rims are often the areas most liable to damage. Acid can be used to disguise damage by re-frosting glass that was originally frosted. Protruding parts, such as beaks on small birds and fingers on figures, and so on, are also vulnerable. Genuine pieces will exhibit a faint mould line extending from the rim to the base – beware of pieces where the base is so highly polished that the mould line is not apparent.

Marks

Most wares are marked "R Lalique", often with "France" in matching script and a model number. The "L" was sometimes elongated. The signature "R. LALIQUE" was also used. Pieces made after 1950, are signed in script "Lalique France", without the initial "R", which was only used during Lalique's lifetime.

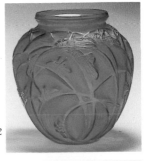

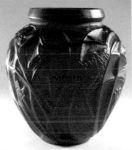

Fakes

Lalique glass has been much faked. Modern fakes are very poor. Those made in the 1920s and 30s are better but can usually be detected by close examination. The genuine Lalique electric blue moulded glass vase, *above, top* has the form, colour and style of decoration readily associated with Lalique. The red vase, *above, bottom*, although similar in form and decoration, is a fake. The most obvious flaw is the colour – one never used by Lalique. The rim is too thick. Many of these fakes bear a wide stencilled mark in relief, with some distance between each letter – not a characteristic of Lalique's marks. The fakes tend to be fairly lightweight. Opalescence, where used, is often all-over, rather than controlled.

RENÉ LALIQUE (2)

Lalique was a prolific designer and his output consisted of an enormous range of items. Pieces with figural subjects are the most popular, followed by insects, animals, geometric motifs, floral wares, and fish.

Car mascots
Car mascots were made in 29 designs. Birds and animals are common subjects, showing either just the head, or the complete creature. Others depict nude female figures. They are usually in clear and frosted glass, sometimes polished. A few are in clear tinted glass. The car mascots that come up most frequently for sale are:
* *St Christophe*
* *Archer*
* *Coq Nain* (a cockerel)
* *Perche* (a fish)
* *Grand Libellule* (a dragonfly)
* *Tête d'Aigle* (an eagle's head)
* *Sanglier* (a wild boar)
* *Chrysis* (a kneeling nude)
* *Longchamps* (a horse's head)
* *Cinq Chevaux* (five rearing horses)
* *Tête de Paon* (a peacock's head)
* *Victoire* (a female head).

Perfume bottles
Lalique's earliest scent bottles were commissioned by Francois Côty. These are usually crisply moulded panel forms; the emphasis is on the decorative stopper. Later, Lalique produced perfume bottles for many of the top parfumiers, including Molinard and Roger & Gallet. The most inventive forms are in greatest demand, and those with the "tiara" stopper are also very collectable. Many bottles and stoppers were made in a choice of colours. Sealed bottles with orginal contents and cartons are always at a premium. Bottles in solid colours are also desirable. More than one stopper was designed for some bottles — check with the 1932 catalogue (see previous page). The underside of the stopper should bear a number corresponding to that on the base.
* Some very small scent bottles carry the initials "RL" instead of a full signature.

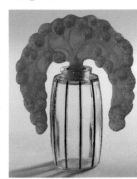
Scent bottle with tiara stopper

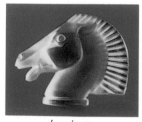
Tête de Paon

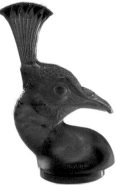
Longchamps

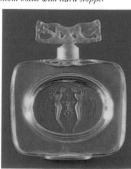
Figural scent bottle

Vases

Lalique made a number of highly decorative vases; these were designed as pieces of sculpture and were never intended to hold flowers.

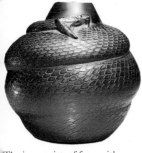

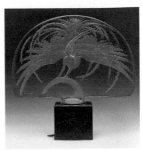

The integration of form with decoration is particularly striking in this famous serpent vase, which was issued in a range of colours, including amber. Typically for Lalique vases, the design is in high relief.

Lamps

Lalique made wall lights, chandeliers, ceiling bowls and table lamps. The table lamps often have highly inventive forms – for example, one has a form similar to that of the tiara-stoppered perfume bottle. Others contain figural decoration. Some, like that shown above, are mounted on bronze bases.

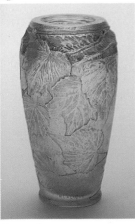

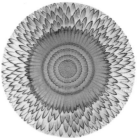

Tablewares

Like the vases, the tablewares are primarily decorative. The shell bowls were the most popular items. The survival rate of Lalique glasses is poor as they were invariably of very thin glass.

Cire-perdue

Glass items, such as the vase shown above, made by the *cire perdue* ("lost wax") method, a casting process which results in unique casts, were the only wares actually made by Lalique, rather than by the workshop to his design. They are thus eagerly sought after, especially as they are unique – the mould has to be broken in order to retrieve the glass. As well as his wheelcut signature, these wares often carry the last two numerals of the year preceded by a serial number.

Jewelry

Lalique's finest jewelry belongs to the Art Nouveau period. Very few of the glass creations survive as they are so vulnerable. Many pieces are in bright colours, such as the electric blue of the bracelet *above* (an effect sometimes achieved by using a coloured foil back). Coloured glass is often used in preference to precious stones.

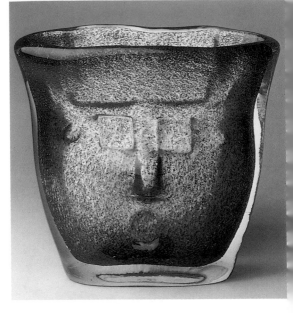

*An intenally decorated glass vase by Maurice Marinot
1926; ht 9in/22.5cm; value code B*

Identification checklist for Marinot glass
1. Is the piece heavy in form?
2. Has the glass been treated as a sculptural medium?
3. Is there an emphasis on internal decoration?
4. Is the design encased in a heavy clear glass surround?
5. Does the piece have an engraved signature, and a number (which may be applied to a paper label attached to the base)?
6. Is there an attempt at tightly controlled use of decorative effect?

Maurice Marinot (French 1882-1960)
A trained technician, chemist and painter, Marinot became fascinated with glass when he visited the glassworks of his friends, the Viard brothers, Eugéne and Gabriel. At first he did designs which they executed but then took to glassmaking himself. All his glass was hand-made using no mass-production moulded techniques. Many pieces have a clear-grey or pale yellow tint. He was not prolific; consequently his work is relatively hard to find and because of its quality as well as its scarcity is invariably expensive.

Signatures
Marinot's work usually bears an engraved signature. The vase shown above is signed "Marinot" and is numbered 1239 on a paper label attached to the base. The base of the perfume bottle, right, also carries an engraved signature.

Decorative techniques

Marinot was primarily interested in the decorative possibilities of glass, especially the way in which imperfections could be turned to decorative advantage. Although his internal decoration appears random, it is in fact finely controlled. At first he worked with enamels, c.1915-18; he then experimented with bubbles, etching and wheel carving, using deep incisions. He also employed deep acid cutting, contrasting a polished upper surface and a granular or frosted lower surface. In the early to mid-20s he shaped the glass at the furnace, using the hot technique to experiment more with form (for example, by the inclusion of metallic oxides, such as tin foil), and dispensed altogether with surface decoration. Some wares incorporate a face or a stylized mask – as for example, in the vase shown on the previous page.

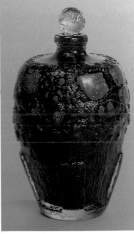

Even small pieces, like this scent bottle, are heavy in form. This example has Marinot's characteristic simple ball stopper: stoppers are nearly always in clear glass although they may be given a decorative surface treatment, as here.

Similar wares

The most successful of those craftsmen who emulated Marinot were Henri Navarre and André Thuret, whose work is collectable and relatively affordable.

CHARLES SCHNEIDER
(French, dates unknown)

One of the glassmakers to whom Marinot's highly individual style appealed was Charles Schneider. Although Schneider's glass does not fare well in direct comparison with Marinot's, much of his work is nevertheless attractive and collectable in its own right, and is far more affordable.

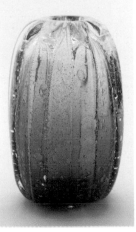

This vase makes an instructive comparison with the work of Marinot. It shows Schneider's preference for heavily walled moulded forms and for an irregular, trapped bubble effect. The result is not as successful as in Marinot's work: the decoration appears truly random, rather than intentionally so, and the decoration and form are not so well integrated. The control over tinting is somewhat loose and the form relatively conventional, without any sculptural quality. Schneider did not tend to use acid cutting. Pieces are signed with the stencilled signature "SCHNEIDER", which on this vase runs vertically up from the base. Many Schneider wares are signed "Le Verre Francais", or "CHARDER".
* The moulded lozenges on the base and around the rim are not features found in Marinot's work.
* Schneider also made cameo glass and internally mottled opaque glass, lampshades and table lamps, some of which resemble work by Daum (see pp. 46-7).

THE DAUM FACTORY

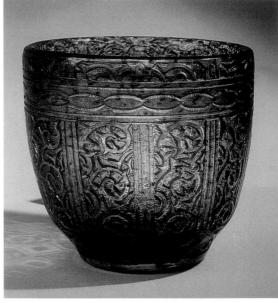

A Daum glass bowl
c.1930; ht 6¹/₂in/17cm; value code C

Identification checklist for Daum etched glass
1. Does the piece make use of all-over decoration?
2. Is it signed, probably on the footrim?
3. Is the surface grainy and uneven?
4. Is the decoration abstract?
5. Is the form fairly heavy and thick-walled, giving a robust impression?

Value point
The hand-made pieces of the early Art Deco years fetch more than those from the industrial period of the later 20s and 30s.

Authenticity
Fakers have yet to turn their attention to Daum glass. Wares are usually signed (see **The Daum Factory**, *opposite*).

Condition
The rims of Daum glass are usually gently rounded. A sharp edge might indicate that a chip has been removed using a polishing wheel. This practice might also be detected by examining the proportions.
46

Fakes
Few fakes have appeared on the market so far, perhaps because the acid-cut wares have been regarded by collectors as less important than the firm's cameo wares. However, some of the lamp forms were copied by some smaller French glassworks, using inferior moulded glass.

Colours
Daum used a few characteristic and distinctive colours, the most common of which are:
* smoky grey
* green
* amethyst
* yellow/amber
* turquoise.

The Daum Factory (French; established 1875).
During the Art Nouveau period (1890-1914) this leading glassworks produced a large quantity of cameo, or overlay, glass, with the naturalistic motifs typical of the period. During the 1920s and 30s the output consisted of mainly etched glass, which soon superseded cameo glass in popularity, although the firm continued to make cameo glass throughout the period. Following closure during the First World War, the factory reopened in 1919 under Paul Daum.

The Daum glassworks embraced Art Deco with enthusiasm during the 1920s, and their lamps, bowls and large decorative vases took an innovative direction. Heavy acid-etched wares with deep decoration predominated. The most popular colours were smoky grey, turquoise, yellow and sea green. Clear glass was also used occasionally. The emphasis was on decorative ornament and irregular, frosted, light-diffusing granular surfaces. Some of these wares were reminiscent of the designs of Marinot (see pp. 44-5). Alternatively, matt and polished surfaces were combined. Decoration, either geometric or floral, tends to be freeform although it may be more formalized, as in the bowl shown here. Most pieces are wheel-engraved with the words "Daum, Nancy" and the insignia, the cross of Lorraine (which was also used by other Nancy glassworks), but wares do not carry the names or initials of individual designers.

Most of the glass of the period is thick-walled and heavy in form. Being robust, it has generally survived well.

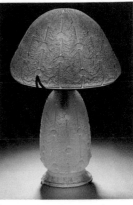

Second only to the vases, lamps were an important part of the factory's output during this period. This etched glass lamp with a frosted white ground and an acid-etched geometric design, is typical. Daum made glass lamps and also supplied glass shades for other lamps, most notably for the wrought-iron bases produced by Edgar Brandt (see pp. 144-5). Heavyweight lead glass was used for hanging and standard lamps. These items were mass-produced, but copied the labour-intensive hand-decorated work of such craftsmen as Décorchement and Argy-Rousseau. From a distance they could be taken for pâte de cristal. Many of the lamps were mushroom-shaped and amber or amethyst with a mottled perimeter in contrasting colours. Surfaces were matt. They usually carry a wheel- or acid-cut signature.
* The heavy forms of acid-etched glass produced by Lalique during the 1920s and 30s are similar to those of Daum.

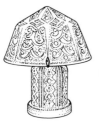 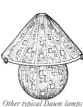 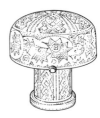

Other typical Daum lamps

Examining Daum glass lamps
If possible, remove the metal mount and examine the neck of the base under a strong light – when the lamp is on the heat can cause the glass to crack. Internal cracks may not be readily apparent.

GABRIEL ARGY-ROUSSEAU

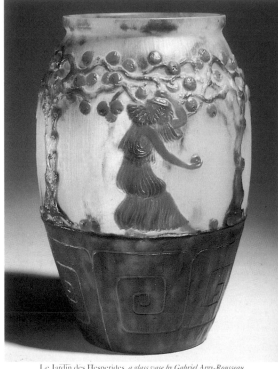

Le Jardin des Hesperides, *a glass vase by Gabriel Argy-Rousseau c.1925; ht 10¹/₂in/24cm; value code C*

Identification checklist for Argy-Rousseau glass
1. Is the piece fairly small?
2. Is it pâte de verre (or more rarely, pâte de cristal)?
3. Is the decoration figural?
4. Is the glass relatively opaque?
5. Does the piece have a moulded signature?
6. Is the base moulded, but without visible mould lines?
7. Are rich colours employed?
8. Is the piece thin-walled and therefore relatively light for its size?

Marks
All Argy-Rousseau's pieces are incised with his mark, which usually appears in one of the following variations: his initials, or "G. ARGY-ROUSSEAU" in capital letters (as in the vase *opposite*), or in upper and lower case letters (G.Argy-Rousseau) as in the vase *above*.
48

Recognition points
Argy-Rousseau's pieces tend to be relatively small – most are under 9 inches (23cm) high (although the example *above* is slightly taller). They are also surprisingly light in weight, even allowing for their small size and the fact that they are made from thin-walled glass.

Gabriel Argy-Rousseau (French, 1885-1953)

Initially a maker of false teeth, Argy-Rousseau first exhibited his pâte de verre in 1914, and from 1919 onward made a series of enamelled scent bottles.

In 1921 he went into partnership with Gustave-Gaston Moser-Millot, who funded a workshop called Les Pâtes-de-verre d'Argy-Rousseau, where several dozen workers produced glassware designed by Argy-Rousseau and sold in Moser-Millot's shop.

As well as vases and scent bottles, Argy-Rousseau made table lamps, bowls, jars, pendants, brooches and perfume burners. In 1928 he produced a group of pâte de cristal sculptures designed by Marcel Bouraine.

Production slowed after 1929, and in 1931 the glassworks were closed. Argy-Rousseau then worked on his own, making commissioned plaques of a religious nature (not popular with collectors) and angular vessels in streaked, jewel-like colours.

Pâte de verre

This type of glass was popular in the Art Nouveau and Art Deco periods. It was made from a paste of powdered glass to which coloured glass or metallic oxides were added to provide colour. The mixture was then fired in a mould to give it shape. The procedure had a fairly high failure rate as the mould could break under heat or the paste fail to gel.

The colours were fused into the glass leaving no visible joints or overlays (unlike cameo glass, whose surface exhibits traces of carving). However, pâte de verre always has an element of hand trimming. There is sometimes evidence of internal mottling because control over pigments is not as precise as with cameo works. The most successful pieces have a degree of translucency.

Pâte de cristal

This was a method developed by Argy-Rousseau and favoured by Décorchement (see pp. 50-1). It is similar to pâte de verre but is made by adding an aqueous adhesive before subjecting the mould to an extended firing at a lower temperature; this makes the colour easier to control and results in a translucent, richly coloured vessel.

Collecting

During the period when Les Pâtes-de-verre d'Argy-Rousseau was operating, from 1921 to 1931, glasswares were produced in large quantities. The moulds were reusable but the pieces had to be coloured by hand and individually finished. Argy-Rousseau's later work is rarer. He is probably the most accomplished maker of pâte de verre and pâte de cristal. His Classical vases of Egyptian inspiration and those depicting prowling wolves are considered the ultimate pieces among collectors, who have recently paid large sums for such items.

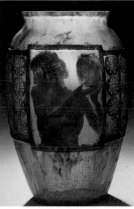

Egyptian motifs, like the maidens on this vase from c.1925, were commonly incorporated into Argy-Rousseau's wares. The use of figural decoration is also characteristic, although he depicted a wide range of subjects including stylized flowers, fruit, birds, animals, butterflies, and some rigidly geometric motifs. Other figural subjects are taken from mythology. His pâte de cristal often features Neo-classical relief decoration.

Colours and finishes

Argy-Rousseau's pieces are usually richly coloured. He favoured white against tortoiseshell to simulate shell cameo, and also mottled pinks against frosted ice reserves. Green was also used.

Note

Those wares designed by Bouraine (see pp. 110-11) include Bouraine's incise-cast signature.

FRANÇOIS-ÉMILE DÉCORCHEMENT

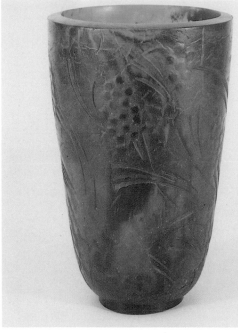

A pâte de cristal vase by François-Émile Décorchement
c.1928; ht 9¹/₂in/24cm; value code C

Identification checklist for glass by Décorchement
1. Is the item either pâte de cristal (partially translucent) or pâte de verre (dense and opaque)?
2. Is it heavy in form?
3. Is there an incise-cast signature?
4. Are the colours bright – perhaps green or blue – and jewel-like?
5. Does the decoration contain either stylized subjects from nature (perhaps a snake), or Cubist or geometric images?
6. Is there an emphasis on internal colours?

François-Emile Décorchement (French, 1880-1971)
Having first trained as a ceramist, Décorchement began to experiment with pâte de verre glass, and then, in 1910, turned to the thicker, more richly coloured, pâte de cristal. From 1915 to 1926 he worked for Lalique, before setting up by himself at the Cristalleries de Saint-Rémy, to make various kinds of moulded
50
glass. He became one of the most important exponents of pâte de verre (see p. 49), but worked predominantly in pâte de cristal, concentrating on heavy forms, with a strong emphasis on internal colours and with the decoration deeply moulded (or engraved) on the exterior. By the 1930s he had turned away from art glassware to concentrate on decorated window panels.

Recognition points

Décorchement is known for a spectrum of particularly bright, jewelled colours which he developed using metallic oxides. Rather than creating tonal variations, he sought to produce uniform coloration, but, as in the vase *opposite*, he would often marble the colours with black or purple to simulate semi-precious stones.

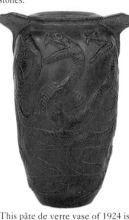

This pâte de verre vase of 1924 is typical of Décorchement's progression from the floral and symbolist themes of the Art Nouveau towards to a bolder, more stylized look that featured flowers, fruit, animals and masks. He particularly favoured the serpent motif, shown in this vase. The use of repeat patterns and motifs is characteristic of Décorchement's work of this period, as is the shaping of the handles in the form of snakes' heads.
* After 1928 Décorchement's style became more chunky and cubistic in form, and the decoration (which was mostly in relief) highly abstract and geometric.

Marks

Décorchement's pieces carry an incise-cast signature.

Condition

Pâte de verre and pâte de cristal items should be examined carefully, as the media lend themselves well to skillful reductions of ears and other projections in order to remove signs of damage. This seriously reduces the value.

ALMARIC WALTER
(French, 1859-1942)

Like Décorchement, Walter began as a ceramist. In 1908 he joined the Daum workshops, where he made pâte de verre decorative wares, before setting up his own glassworks in 1919. He also produced a number of designs created by other Daum designers such as the sculptor Henri Berge, and local artists.

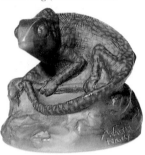

Walter's work is highly sculptural, as in the pâte de verre chameleon illustrated, *above*, dating from 1920. His style retained many elements of the Art Nouveau influence, and featured a variety of naturalistic motifs including small reptiles such as the one shown here: frogs, insects and goldfish were also favoured. His pieces often show a keen control of colour – for example, the salamander is spotted for a more realistic effect. Walter also made pâte de verre medallions, wall sconces and decorative panels, but the mainstays of his output were the small useful or decorative pieces such as ashtrays, pin trays, brooches and pendants.
* Almaric Walter's pâte de verre is relatively heavy and opaque and usually includes more than one colour.

Marks

Pieces produced before 1914 are marked "DAUM NANCY" with the Cross of Lorraine. After 1919, Walter's work is signed "AW" or "A. WALTER, NANCY"; the designer's signature is sometimes included as well. The mark or signature usually appears on the decorated surface at the side of the piece, rather than on the base, which is often ground to a smooth flat finish.
* Fakes can be identified by their uninspiring colours.

BACCARAT

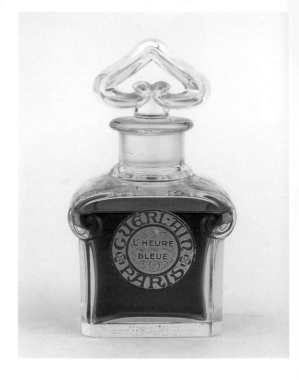

L'Heure Bleue, *Baccarat perfume bottle produced for Guerlain 1912; value code G*

Identification checklist for Baccarat perfume bottles
1. Is the decoration largely confined to the stopper?
2. Is the piece well-moulded?
3. Is the design restrained, with a Neo-classical or geometric influence?
4. Does the stopper incorporate a dropper?
5. Is the piece in clear glass?
6. Is the decoration either intaglio-moulded or (more rarely) enamelled?
7. Do the stopper and bottle belong together (see Beware, *opposite*)?
8. Is it signed?

Marks
The bottles are marked on the base with an acid-etched mark or a stencilled circle mark incorporating a central decanter and stopper flanked by a tumbler and wine glass. The firm's 19thC-style moulded lustre vases usually incorporated the name "Baccarat", moulded in low relief. Wares do not carry the names of individual designers. The work of this firm is not known to have been faked, although the perfume bottles were widely copied.

Baccarat (French, founded 1764)

Baccarat designed bottles for a number of parfumiers, including d'Orsay, Jean Patou, Rimmel, Yardley, Elizabeth Arden, Coty, Roger & Gallet, Lentheric and Guerlain. In the 20s and 30s, under the influence of the sculptor George Chevalier, the emphasis was on enamelling, and on geometric motifs and panel forms with sharp edges. Cut and moulded forms were also used, and there was often some decorative staining.
* Other leading French scent bottle designers were Süe et Mare and the Italian Elsa Schiaparelli. Perhaps the most inventive designs were those of René Lalique (see p. 40).

Beware

Many of the stoppers incorporate an integral dropper; this is often damaged or missing. A danger with these bottles is that a Baccarat stopper may have been matched up with a bottle to which it does not belong: collectors should always examine the proportions and fit of any bottle and stopper, and also try to familiarize themselves with the types made by a given factory. Books are still in print today that catalogue the output of specific firms (see pp. 186-7).

Value point

Provided that they have survived intact, perfume bottles with atomizers ususally command higher prices than those without.

CZECH BOTTLES

The new demand in the scent trade for inexpensive perfume bottles was to a large extent satisfied by Czech glassworks: there were over 50 glassworks in Czechoslovakia during the 20s and 30s making mass-produced (rather than commissioned) glass perfume bottles. Much of the glass tends to be relatively poorly moulded. However, the bottles are increasingly collectable, and relatively inexpensive. The more inventive the design and the more they exemplify the Art Deco style, the more desirable (and costly) they are. Czech bottles are seldom marked, and as they are not highly individualistic, it is hard to distinguish between the various makers and factories. Styles are often reminiscent of French bottles, although the Czech designers did not actually copy French designs, as had been suggested. The tinted and enamelled bottles resemble those of Baccarat.

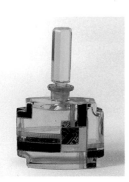

The use of black and clear enamel is reminiscent of some designs by Baccarat, but although attractive, this Czech bottle lacks the delicacy of the French pieces – for example, compare the crisp edges of the Baccarat bottle on the facing page, with the relatively heavy edges of this example. (See also p. 63.)

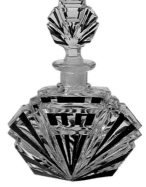

This Czech bottle is among the best of those produced and will command a relatively high price: its striking fan-shaped form, nicely complemented by the stopper, is absolutely characteristic of the period. It is well moulded and attention has been paid to the intricate decoration.

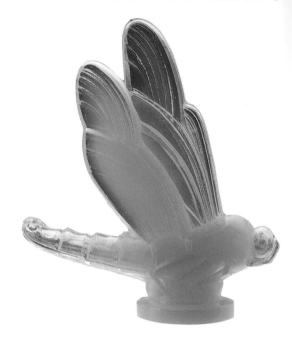

*A moulded glass dragonfly car mascot by Sabino
c.1935; ht 5in/12.5cm; value code F*

Identification checklist for Sabino glass

1. Is the glass moulded?
2. Is the piece opalescent throughout if tableware or a light fitting; or is the opalescence localized if a figure?
3. Are the mould lines evident?
4. If the piece is figural, are the female subjects stylized, with soft features and long legs?
5. If the glass is coloured is it blue, creamy white or pale amber?

Marius-Ernest Sabino
(French, 1878-1961)

From c.1923 until the closure of the glassworks in 1939, Sabino made a range of glass tablewares and car mascots, many of them in a style that is strongly reminiscent of Lalique. However, the designs were intended for mass-production and as such were less expensive. Although competently executed and relatively attractive, most of his work is recognizably inferior when compared with that of Lalique. However, certain pieces withstand comparison and are worth collecting, especially some of his figural wares and his ceiling lights. Some of his lighting fixtures were commissioned for the *Normandie* liner (see p. 9).

Note

Sabino is a minefield for collectors. Experience in observing and handling opalescent glass from the 1920s and 30s may help in detecting a modern piece.

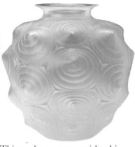

This opalescent vase with a hint of blue, is among the least desirable of Sabino wares, being somewhat clumsy and ill-proportioned. As with his car mascots, the quality of draftsmanship is poor, especially in comparison with Lalique wares, and the mould lines are very evident.

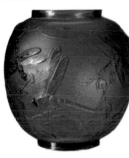

Sabino has been accused of a lack of imagination in finding new motifs, instead borrowing images from other designers, especially Lalique, and rendering them in a clumsy way. Nevertheless, even where using a familiar motif such as the dragonfly, Sabino occasionally achieved a pleasing synthesis of form and decoration. The dragonfly vase, *above*, from 1930 represents the upper range of his work. Here, the dragonfly motif is more finely executed than that of the car mascot, *opposite*, and the piece is delicate and well-proportioned.

Signatures
Sabino signed his work in a variety of ways. The most usual form of signature was moulded. The engraved signature, which usually appears on pieces from the 1930s, takes the form of a large "S", with the rest of the name appearing in small script letters.

Later reproductions
Many of the moulds in which Sabino's designs were executed, were re-used when the factory reopened. It can be difficult to tell which period a piece belongs to, as none of Sabino's work is dated or numbered. However, the more modern wares are likely to be less restrained in their use of opalescence than the earlier ones. Compare the piece under consideration with one known to be from the 20s or 30s. Production ceased in 1975, although an American firm continued to make Sabino wares using the original moulds. These items carry a paper label which says "Sabino, made in France", but if this is missing the only way to determine the date is to examine the piece for signs of natural wear.

EDMUND ETLING ET CIE
(French, active 1920s and 30s)

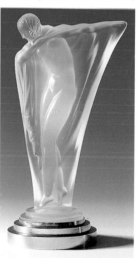

Opalescent glass was also made by Etling. In addition to figures of female nudes, the firm made opalescent glass models of animals and ships, as well as a number of moulded vases, frequently of greyish glass with alternate polished and matt sections. The gold-coloured body of this opalescent figurine, c.1925, is cloaked in folds rendered in a characteristic pale bluish tint.
* Etling also commissioned and retailed bronze and ivory statuettes by a number of leading designers.

55

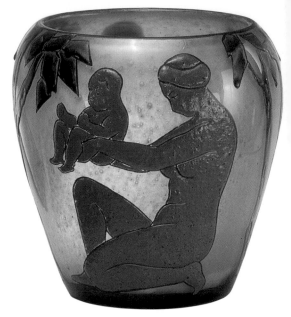

A Marcel Goupy enamelled glass figural vase
c.1925; ht 7in/18cm; value code D

Identification checklist for Goupy glass
1. Is the decoration enamelled?
2. Is the form very simple?
3. Does the decoration show a balanced use of colour and an avoidance of harsh or garish tones?
4. Is the rim finished with a fine enamel trim?
5. Is the glass relatively thick-walled?
6. Is the glass hand-blown?
7. Is the piece signed, the signature applied to a polished pontil mark on the base (where the glass was formed on the pontil rod)?

Recognition point
The glass base is often an important feature of Goupy's glassware and the decoration is sympathetic to the body – distinguishing it from much other French glassware on which the enamel decoration is so thick that it obscures the base.

Signatures
All the designs executed by Heiligenstein (see facing page) bear Goupy's signature in enamel,

but some items made by the firm are unsigned – for example, the jazz band tumbler opposite, although it is fairly certainly attributed to Goupy.

Condition
Goupy's enamelled glasswares tend to have survived in good condition, (unlike those of Ena Rottenberg, see facing page), as the enamels, which were evenly applied, are well fused with the glass.

Marcel Goupy (French, 1886-1954 retd)

Goupy was artistic director at La Maison Geo. Rouard from 1909 until 1954, and designed both forms and decoration. He concentrated on a range of mostly small utilitarian enamelled glasswares, including drinking glasses, boxes, decanters and vases. From the end of the 1920s some of his glasswares were engraved. He also did some designs for ceramics, occasionally to match glasswares, but also as independent pieces or sets, or for ceramics firms, such as Sèvres. Favoured motifs include nudes, landscapes, birds and flowers, and some mythological scenes. From c.1925, in common with the work of other designers, motifs became somewhat more geometric.
* Between 1919 and 1923 the enamelled decoration that appeared on many of his designs was executed by a young French glassworker, Auguste Heiligenstein.

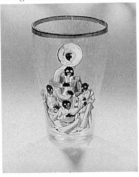

Although he used bright colours, Goupy avoided the garishness that characterizes much glassware of the period, especially some Bohemian glass, which tended to adopt a Clarice Cliff-style brightness and made use of sharp contrasts. The colours of the jazz band tumbler, *above*, are restricted in range and the rim trim echoes the hues of the main design. The figures are characteristically stylized. The form and hand-enamelled decoration would have been designed by Goupy but not executed by him.
* Glasses and other items of the period that are decorated with Negro musicians or nightclub scenes tend to command a premium.

ENA ROTTENBERG (Austrian, dates unknown)

A very distinctive type of enamelled glass was produced by E. Rottenberg in Austria. Wares are invariably small – even vases are seldom taller than a foot (30cm). Light and shade are cleverly used to create a three-dimensional tableau effect. Rottenberg concentrated on vases. The glass, which is hand-blown, and usually thin-walled and relatively light, is not of high quality, and often shows a pontil mark on the underside. The base is usually thick. Pieces are unsigned and do not carry the mark of the firm Loebmeyer, who executed many of the designs.

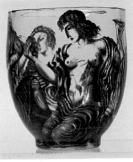

Rottenberg's subjects are predominantly female, as in the piece *above*, and are often semi-naked and depicted in a classical pose. They tend to have a highly stylized face with a pronounced nose, deep-set eyes and high cheek bones. Typically, the rim is untrimmed.
* Unsigned glasswares, similarly decorated but with skin tones, have also been attributed to Rottenberg.

JEAN LUCE (French, 1865-1964)

Another important designer of enamel-decorated glasswares, mostly with floral or geometric motifs, was the Frenchman Jean Luce. Some of his designs were also quite stylized. Like Goupy, he made matching tablewares and glasswares. Later work was abstract and experimental, and made use of a variety of techniques, including acid-etching. Some pieces are reminiscent of the work of Marinot, especially those with contrasting smooth and rough surfaces.

ORREFORS

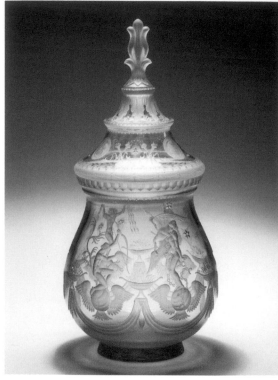

An Orrefors engraved bowl and cover
1937; ht 17in/43.5cm; value code D

Identification checklist for Orrefors glass
1. Does the decoration convey a sense of movement or fluidity?
2. Is the form inventive?
3. Does the form complement the subject of the decoration – for example, are underwater scenes on rippled glass?
4. Are any women in the decoration stylized and muscular, with athletic postures?
5. Is the piece signed?
6. Is the design engraved or frosted, and possibly encased between layers of glass?
7. Is the glass clear, perhaps with a faint blue tint, or a pale smoky effect?

Simon Gate (Swedish, 1883-1945)
Gate was the leading designer at Orrefors from 1917. His work is readily distinguished from that of

the other engravers at Orrefors by its employment of deep surface engraving, Neo-classical style and muscular stylized figures, more often women than men.

Tints

Much of the glass produced by the company, especially in the 1920s, is very subtly tinted although on first inspection it appears clear. An Orrefors tint can often be discerned around the rim when the piece is turned on edge. The cup and cover, *left*, has a strong smoky amethyst tint.

Orrefors (Swedish, founded 1898)

The factory made utilitarian wares, but it is the innovative engraved or internally decorated wares that are the most collectable today.

Their engraved glassware reveals a pleasure in devising inventive decoration, with pieces decorated on both sides to give a three-dimensional effect. Popular motifs are engraved nudes, Neo-classical scenes, and legends. The clear delicate glasswares, with scant decoration, mostly belong to the 1920s.

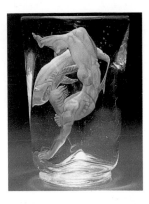

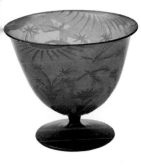

The firm is best known for its Graal wares (from the Swedish for Holy Grail), developed by Simon Gate in 1916 and refined during the 1920s. They were made using a kind of cameo technique by which the design is etched onto the glass and then encased in a clear outer layer. Early Graal is often tinted; orange-brown was particularly popular. The Graal glass vase *above*, designed by Edvard Hald and executed by Knut Bergkvist in 1928, is typical in the way it incorporates colours into the decoration and in the impression it gives of fluidity and mobility. It is engraved "Graal 1928 KB-EH" and numbered 3112.
* Hald's designs are more up-to-the-minute than Gate's and often not as deeply etched.

Orrefors glass of the 1930s was heavier than it had been in the 20s, and designs became bolder and more emphatic, with a greater degree of stylization. Many of the mermaids and sub-aqua scenes, like that shown on the glass vase *above*, engraved by Vicke Lindstrand c.1930, were produced in this decade. Lindstrand, who had a more Modernist approach than Gate, joined the firm in 1927/8. In the 1930s he developed "Ariel" glass, manipulating the glass to create unusual effects, for example, to suggest the undulating surface of water by trapping air bubbles between layers of clear glass and forming them into patterns. Edvard Hald and Edvin Ohrstrom (a designer at Orrefors from 1936 to 47) also favoured this technique.

Marks and output

Production was relatively limited. Until 1930 only about 1,500 pieces were produced and just over one third of these were made before the end of the First World War. There is a wealth of information on the base of pieces: usually they are engraved with "Orrefors" or "O.f.m" and with the name of the designer and engraver, and often with a year code and shape number as well.

Collecting Orrefors

Although it has become more expensive in the last few years, Orrefors glass still represents a good investment. As the body is usually relatively thick and robust, and the pieces were treated as decorative cabinet wares, they tend to be in good condition with little sign of wear.

STEUBEN GLASSWORKS

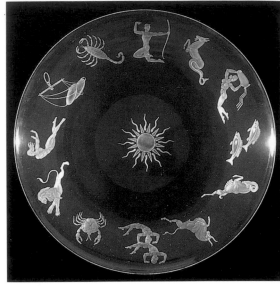

*A zodiac platter by Sidney Waugh
c.1938; dia. 16in/41cm; value code C*

Identification checklist for the glassware designed by
Sidney Waugh and Walter Dorwin Teague for Steuben
Glassworks
1. If a figural piece, are the figures highly stylized?
2. If the piece is engraved, is the engraving quite fine?
3. Is the piece marked?
4. Is the form quite restrained?
5. Is the crystal unusually pure and clear?

Note
During the 1930s most of the recognizably Art Deco work was
produced by Sidney Waugh and Walter Dorwin Teague, rather than by
Frederick Carder, whose work was more traditional.

Steuben Glass works
(American, 1903-present)
The company was founded in
1903 by the Englishman
Frederick Carder, and became a
division of Corning in 1918. In the
United States its work is regarded
as the epitome of elegance in Art
Deco glass. Before 1930 Carder
designed many items himself, but
from 1930 onward the company
employed a number of leading
designers.

From 1933 the company
produced only items of colourless
pure crystal, concentrating on
massive vessels with swelling

fluid forms complemented by
engraved designs.

Marks
It is important to be aware of the
various marks used, as the
company is still in operation
today, producing mainly
tablewares. Steuben glass made
between 1903 and 1932 is usually
acid-stamped on the base with a
fleur-de-lys and the word
"Steuben" on a scroll. After 1932
the word Steuben or just "S" was
engraved with a diamond point.
The name of the designer is not
usually included.

Sidney Waugh (American, 1904-63)

Waugh was Chief Associate Designer for Steuben Glassworks from 1933 until his death. In the 1930s he developed a range of crystalware inspired by traditional, mythological themes, such as the zodiac glass platter *opposite*, which clearly shows his use of elongated, highly stylized monumental figures and sleek animals, crisply engraved to give the impression of bas-relief.

* The influence of Scandanavian design is evident in the restrained style of much of Teague's and Waugh's work, especially the tableware (including the pieces shown here). Waugh in particular was influenced by the glassmasters of Orrefors (see pp. 58-9).

* Many of Waugh's works were issued in limited edition pieces and may bear engraved series numbers.

Walter Dorwin Teague (American, 1883-1960)

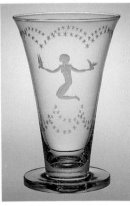

Teague is best known for his industrial designs, which include cars, cameras and pens. The colourless blown and engraved ice tea glass, *above*, c.1932, is from the brief period during which he was employed by Steuben to create a range of five or so patterns of elegant, functional crystal stemware.

Frederick Carder (English, 1863-1963)

Carder was an able designer, and, until he left Steuben in 1930, designed many of the firm's finest items himself. Initially his influences were strongly European and rooted in his 19thC training, His work remained relatively conservative although he adopted aspects of the new 1920s style, such as rhythmic curves and zigzags, clearly influenced by French Art Deco designs, including the work of René Lalique.

Carder developed a number of innovative techniques, including Aurene ware (see below).

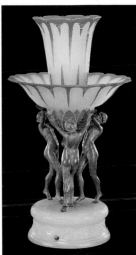

Carder's coloured glass continued European design traditions. His work uses brilliant colours and organic shapes, typified by this 1920s bronze and acid-etched alabaster glass lamp.

* Between 1934, when he retired from Steuben, and 1959, Carder worked independently and concentrated on casting glass in the *cire perdue* technique (meaning "lost wax", the French term for a casting process that results in unique glass casts). Most pieces are signed.

"Aurene" ware

This line of iridescent glass in various colours, particularly gold and blue, was made between 1904 and 1933 in a variety of forms, including vases and candlesticks, with a classical or Art Nouveau influence. The style did not vary greatly during the 29 years of its production, and pieces are therefore difficult to date.

MINOR GLASS

Most inexpensive glass from the 1920s and 30s is moulded and often geometric in form. Female nudes were the most popular motifs. Much of the work available uses debased Lalique designs; this is especially true of glass produced by the lesser French and Czech glassworks and also some manufacturers from North-East England. However, interest has revived recently in the cloud glass made in England by Davidson's and in the "Chippendale" glass the firm produced from American designs. Some attempts were made at producing British art glass by Mrs Graydon-Stannus, and also, after 1924, by the Monart Works in Perth. Several Venetian glassworks at Murano, notably Vennini and Salviati, made a number of figurines of dancing maidens, often in opaque white glass and supported on black hoop bases.

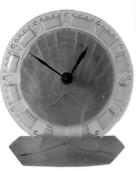

This desk clock, only 8-9in high (20-23cm), was made as an advertising piece. It has an image of the liner, the *Normandie*, in the centre, with the sun's rays, a typical decorative feature of the time, behind it. The letters of the liner's name appear in the place of numerals. It is not of outstanding technical or decorative merit, but anything from the *Normandie* is collectable.

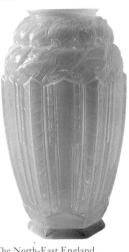

The North-East England company Jobling and Co produced machine-made pressed glass in a similar style to that of Sabino (see pp. 54-5). In 1933 the firm introduced a range of art glass using French-inspired designs, including a limited number of opalescent wares such as this vase. The high gloss surface is typical, but the design is not very successful, and the form is uninteresting. Nevertheless, these wares are collectable.

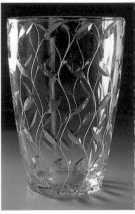

This engraved vase is Brierley crystal, a variety of English glassware. The designers, Clyne Farquharson and Keith Murray, introduced more modern decorative elements into the work of a range of factories that had been producing mainly fussy, opulent brilliant-cut lead crystal glassware in Victorian patterns, popular at the beginning of the century. Although this example is attractive, it remains a compromise between tradition and modernity.

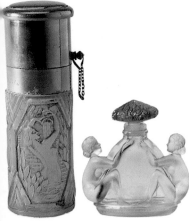

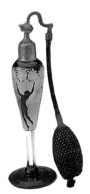

Atomizers often imitate designs by Lalique: this one, in pressed glass , resembles those he made for Molinard. The mechanisms are usually the same, although Lalique's mounts were all made by one manufacturer. The atomizer in this form was invented in the 1920s and 30s.

Many scent bottles were produced in France (with restrained designs) and Czechoslovakia (often with figural decoration and occasionally with outrageous forms and proportions, but see p. 53). The market is growing for the better ones: the main criteria are quality of execution, and novelty – both features of the French bottle, *above left*, and the Czech example, *above right*. If bottles retain their packaging, and were made for quality perfumes, this adds to their value. Do not assume that any contents are the original perfume, as sometimes bottles are filled with a coloured liquid for display purposes in stores or auction houses.

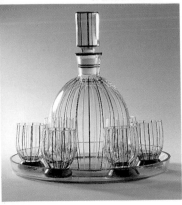

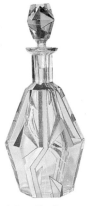

Many of the tablewares that survive from the period are Czech, as these are, *above*, and are unmarked. They tend to imitate French designs: both the decanters here have a Baccarat feel (see pp. 52-3). The silver and black enamel decoration was very popular. These glasses are in unusually good condition, with the enamel intact; it is also rare to find a full set. The single panel-cut decanter is also in unusually good condition, and although the piece is unmarked, the strong design and decoration make it desirable.

CERAMICS

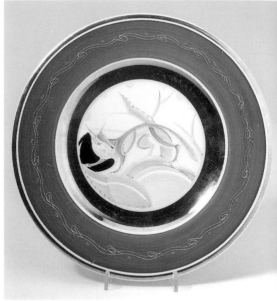

A plate by Susie Cooper (see pp. 78-9) decorated with a stylized fox

Many of the ceramics from the 1920s and 30s available on the market today consist of high-quality work by top designers. At the other end of the market there are many inexpensive tablewares (see pp. 100-1), some of very little merit. Tablewares predominate, and are usually sold as single pieces: it is not necessary to collect sets.

The most influential British potter of the period was Clarice Cliff (see pp. 74-7), whose brightly coloured pieces were produced by the Newport Pottery in Staffordshire. Many of these wares are hybrids of traditional shapes, forms and techniques and more Modernist decorative elements. Cliff had many imitators, and an enormous quantity of Clarice Cliff lookalikes were produced. Other major designers include Susie Cooper (see pp. 68-9) and manufacturers such as Burleigh and Myott, who produced wares in original shapes. However, the output of most British potteries during this period, even those who did try to modernize part of their range, remained essentially traditional.

This period saw a growing use of glaze effects. Lustre wares were made famous by Wedgwood, and were emulated by a number of other firms, including Malling in Newcastle. The Lancastrian Pottery's innovative decorative technique for their Lapis ware used pigment and glaze fused into the body; however, they continued to use traditional forms. By contrast Shelley and Royal Doulton were known for their stark white bone china.

There was a growing market for general ornaments, retailed through seaside shops. Small animal figurines by Sylvac and others found a ready market. Painted chalk figures, especially of the variety showing damsels being walked by borzois, were also popular, but are not regarded as important today. Those which do survive tend to be in poor condition, as chalk blisters in strong sunlight and fractures easily. Cheap Czech Art Deco figurines and glassware were imported into Britain during this period: most of these too are not worth collecting, as they look mass-produced and are often badly made.

In Italy, Gio Ponti produced figures similar to the stylish porcelain and earthenware pieces by the Lenci factory in Turin, as well as tasteful wares for Ginori, in which design and decoration complement one another.

In Germany, Rosenthal (see p. 95) and several other bone china and porcelain manufacturers worked in a clean, classical style, especially in their tablewares. In Vienna, Goebel and Hutchenreuther made figurines. Earthenware was produced by Katzhütte.

In France, Limoges, which employed a number of top designers, continued to be the main centre for mass-produced ceramics, but even there traditional forms provided the mainstay of production. The firms of Robj and Argilor popularized the novelty night-light, which they produced in porcelain, often using Middle Eastern figures such as harem girls and small turbaned boy servants.

Some of the most "modern"-looking pieces produced during this period come from Scandinavia. Interesting animal sculptures by Knud Khyn use stoneware covered with heavy celadon and orange-green glazes.

American ceramics in the Art Deco style are relatively scarce and are either pieces designed by prominent artists in progressive styles and made to high technical and artistic standards, or more readily available French-inspired or "streamline" wares, made for mass consumption during the 1930s. Among the most heavily collected of this second type are the *Fiesta* wares and other products of the Hall China Company, most of which use bright monochrome glazes. Small, geometrically stylized wares by the Rookwood Pottery bear impressed marks, and are mostly finished with matt monochrome glazes. Similar glazes and styles are found on the later products of the Fulper and Weller potteries, most of which bear clear printed marks. A line of highly geometric designed vases with matt, polychrome glazes was sold in the late 1920s by the Roseville pottery in Ohio, under the trademark "Futura". These are of inferior quality but are far more interesting in design than Roseville's earlier wares.

Many wares are marked. Collectors should familiarize themselves with the signatures used during the period by consulting one of the many catalogues and mark books available (see pp. 186-7).

RENÉ BUTHAUD

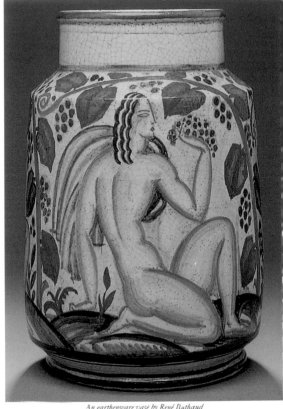

An earthenware vase by René Buthaud
1920s; ht 13in/33cm; value code C

Identification checklist for the ceramics of Buthaud
1. Is the decoration geometric or figural (perhaps depicting a Neo-classical or Negro subject), and linear, with stylized features?
2. Is the form earthenware rather than porcelain?
3. Do any female figures have firm, painted outlines?
4. Is there a painted signature?
5. Does the palette show a preference for blue-grey and/or iron red?
6. Is the ground stone or cream colour?
7. Does the rim have a painted trim?
8. Is the form relatively conventional?

Sgraffito
Buthaud was one of the principal exponents of sgraffito, or carved-away decoration – the word is Italian for "scratched", and refers

to the technique by which a pottery body is dipped in a separate slip of another colour, through which the decoration is then carved.

René Buthaud (French, 1886-1986)

Initially, Buthaud was trained as a silver decorator before going on to study art in Paris. As well as the pottery for which he is mostly remembered, he also did graphics, watercolours and some stained-glass windows designs. Some of his poster designs have the same idealized females with strong outlines that appear on much of his ceramics. The influence of other painters, especially Jean Dupas (see pp. 130-31) and Eugene Robert Pougheon is often evident in his work. Other pieces had Neo-classical imagery.

Buthaud first worked in ceramics after the First World War, and his vases were first exhibited in 1920. He also produced faïence vases with hand-painted figural decoration similar to that used on his painted wares and often with brown or green outlines.

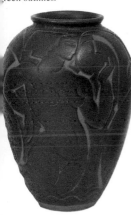

Buthaud's ceramics, which were predominantly vases of simple form, were usually either painted, crackle-glazed or sgrafitto. The earthenware vase *above*, from the 1920s, which is incised with highly stylized mermaids, is typical of his sgrafitto work in its dark, chocolatey-brown tones against a paler underlying earthenware body. The subjects tend to be female, with elongated forms and very stylized faces. Their hair is usually rendered in stylized waves giving a crimped effect.
* The figural decoration on Buthaud's sgrafitto wares often depicts Negroes.

Availability
Buthaud's work is much collected in Paris and New York and to a lesser extent in Britain. He was not prolific, and prices tend to be high. Fakes have not so far appeared on the market, perhaps because of the difficulty of reproducing artificially the signs of age that have invariably built up on the earthenware bases over the years.

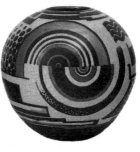

Geometric designs often feature in Buthaud's work. Like the earthenware vase *above*, the geometric wares usually have a brown palette and tend to be decorated in various tones of one main colour. Characteristically, the interlocked curves of this vase accentuate its almost spherical form.
* Buthaud made a number of crackle-glazed earthenware vases. These bear either the painted mark "R. Buthaud", or the incised or painted monogram, "RB". Some have quasi-mythical figures, such as mermaids and fauns; others are decorated with pastoral elements or landscapes.
* The crackled glaze was also used by other potters, such as Boch Frères (pp. 70-1) and Royal Copenhagen.
* In the 1920s and 30s Buthaud was one of the first and most successful of the artists who incorporated African motifs into their work following the success of the *Revue Nègre*.

EMILE LENOBLE (French, 1876-1939)
Emile Lenoble was another leading French studio potter who used the sgraffito technique of decoration on some of his stonewares. Glazes were matt or textured rather than polished. Motifs were usually geometric or floral and stylized.

67

SÈVRES

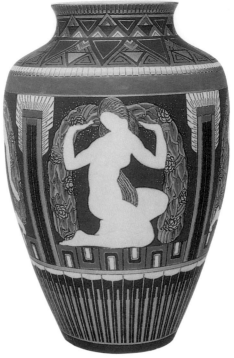

*A huge Sèvres jardinière
1924; ht approx. 2ft/61cm; value code B*

Identification checklist for Sèvres porcelain
1. Is the piece signed?
2. Is it of particularly high quality?
3. Is the form relatively conventional, with any innovative elements in the piece being provided by the decoration?
4. Is the surface heightened in some way, perhaps with gilt or heavy pigment?

Note
* It is particularly difficult to provide an extensive checklist for Sèvres wares in the Art Deco period as the designs are so individual and were executed by a number of designers given free range.

Sèvres (French, established 1750)
Until very recently this factory's Art Deco wares were regarded as the poor relations of their wares made in earlier periods, but in the last two years these items have been receiving as much attention as the much-praised 18thC

porcelain. From 1920 Sèvres was under the direction of Georges LeChevallier-Chévignard. He employed a number of top designers, including some who traditionally worked in other media. The factory's reputation was such that he was able to call upon the top designers of the day,

Decoration and glazes

The porcelain jardinière in the main picture, made in 1924, characterizes much of the output of the factory in the Deco period: the form is large but not otherwise innovative. The emphasis is largely on the elaborate decoration. Egyptian motifs, such as the pillars, the pose of the woman, and the chevron and gold motifs, were very popular at this period. Geometric decoration was also frequently used. Like much work of the period, the main figure is a female nude, simplistically represented, with no painted embellishment. The exceptionally high quality is indicative of Sèvres.

The glaze is matt heightened by gilt. Similar emphasis is placed on the finish of the vase and cover, which has an impasto glaze – that is, mixed with pigment to give a raised effect.

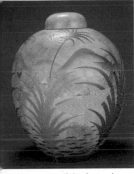

Rapin was one of the factory's leading designers, and designed the form of this massive vase and cover, *Tropiques* in 1925, probably for exhibition at the Paris Exhibition (see pp. 8-9), although the decoration was finally conceived and executed only in 1939 by Anne-Marie Fontaine, a designer who worked at Sèvres between 1928 and 38. Typically of Sèvres designers, her mark appears on the footrim.
* The same vase and cover was also made in plain dark cobalt blue.
* The inventive design and slightly unconventional form of the *Tropiques* vase represent a departure for Sèvres from their usual straightforward, commercially safe shapes adapted from 18thC designs for dinner and tea wares.

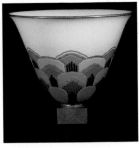

This Sèvres vase, designed by Jacques-Emile Ruhlmann (see pp. 12-3) in 1932, has, for Sèvres, an unusually ornate, even avant-garde form. However, the use of gilt is characteristic of Sèvres wares, as is the harmony achieved between form and decoration: the large expanse of ivory porcelain is juxtaposed with the busy design of overlapping, pale blue, lilac and grey panels.
* The fine detail of the gilt comb and dot ornamentation along the top of the decoration is typical of this craftsman's work generally and is equally apparent in many of his furniture designs (see pp. 12-13).

Other leading Sèvres designers and decorators
Robert Bonfils
Emile Decoeur
Jean Dupas
Anne Marie Fontaine
Suzanne Lalique
Francois Pompon
Taxile Doat

Signatures
Sèvres wares were signed between 1738 and 1954, but signatures should be regarded with caution. At least 80% of 18th and early 19thC porcelain with the Sèvres mark was not made at the factory – many factories producing wares at the same time freely copied the mark. However, in the late 19thC a new system was introduced at Sèvres which showed the letter "S" with the date underneath, contained in a triangle. This particular mark was rarely copied and is seldom faked. Collectors should particularly beware the Sèvres mark that shows two interlaced Ls (the royal cipher) as this is the most commonly faked one. It was introduced in 1739 and a date coding mark was added in 1753.

BOCH FRÈRES

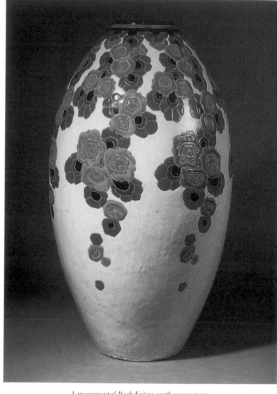

*A monumental Boch Frères earthenware vase
c.1925; ht 5ft 4in/1.63m; value code C*

Identification checklist for Boch Frères ceramics
1. Is the form a large ovoid, perhaps mounted?
2. Are the surface enamels thickly applied?
3. Is there a signature?
4. Have bold primary colours been used?
5. Is the decoration applied over the glaze?
6. If the reserve colour is pale, is it ivory rather than white?
7. Is there a crackle or craquelure, effect under a thick glaze?

Boch Frères

The Belgian firm Boch Frères was founded in 1767 at Sept Fontaines in the Saarland, but by the mid-19thC, following a split, part of the firm established their manufactory, Boch Frères, Keramis, in Belgium. They produced mainly earthenware vases, some tablewares, and candlesticks. Boch Frères wares of the mid-20s-40s represent the most important Belgian contribution to Art Deco. Some stonewares were also produced. Both the earthenware and the stoneware produced by the firm in this period are whitebodied.

A. W. Finch

Along with the leading Keramis designer in the Deco period, Charles Catteau (see right), an early contribution in the period was also made by the English artist Arthur Finch, who worked for Boch Frères as a decorator until 1930. His vases employ the large, swollen design typical of the factory, but he used a red background in slip and glazed ochre to the dark green and blue motifs.

Other crackle wares

The wares produced by Boch Frères are similar in treatment to Czech Amphora wares. These are also heavily enamelled with incised, deeply moulded outlines. Other firms producing wares with crackled glazes beneath painted or enamelled decoration were the French firm Longwy, for Primavera (see pp. 72-3), and the English pottery, Poole (see pp. 86-7), who used a more subtle crackle effect.

Signatures

A number of marks were used on Keramis wares: some pieces are stamped "KERAMIS MADE IN BELGIUM" and carry a painted design number. Others may be stamped "BOCH FES LA LOUVIERE MADE IN BELGIUM FABRICATION BELGE" These may also have a style and pattern number. Alternatively they may bear the painted initials "B.F.K", and a style number. Some pieces also bear the name of the designer: the elephant vase is inscribed "Keramis" with the painted mark "Ch. Catteau D.1082 B.F.K."

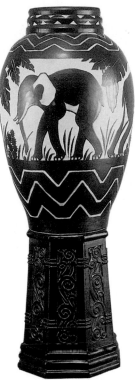

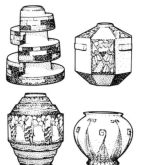

Other innovative Boch Frères vases

Both the elephant vase *above* and the floral one shown opposite were designed by Charles Catteau. The elephant vase typifies his work in its large monumental size (it is 4ft/1.2m high). It is decorated with thickly applied enamel motifs which stand out in relief from the background. This is often of a thickly glazed ivory with a craquelure effect. The choice of an animal in a naturalized setting is characteristic.

Other designs are linear or zigzag, with stylized animals – perhaps penguins or leaping gazelles. Incised stylized flowers pendant from the rim also appear frequently. Favourite colours were deep green, blue, black and brown. Forms could be of a simple ovoid shape, with little or no base and a narrow rim.

Later Catteau designs were more geometrically elaborate – for example, the ovoid form might be extended at the base, as in this vase.

PRIMAVERA

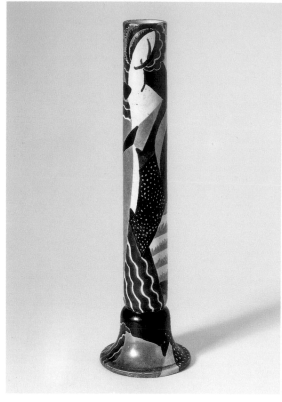

A Primavera vase
c.1925; ht 14in/35.5cm; value code D

Identification checklist for Primavera ceramics
1. Is the item pottery?
2. If it is an animal, is it devoid of colour, relying instead on a monochrome glaze, perhaps crazed?
3. Does it have an incise-moulded signature?
4. Is the decoration stylized?
5. Are the colours subtly blended, with muted glazes?
6. Is the shape avant garde?

Primavera (French, 1920s & 30s)
Primavera was the design studio of the Parisian department store Au Printemps and was one of the leading salons of the Deco period. The firm produced a range of ceramic wares, including figures and simple monochrome animal studies. The vase shown *above* is typical of Primavera, with its stylized, almost unreadable, female figure. (A stylized Negro is depicted on the reverse.) Characteristically, the form is relatively simple but original, with a sculptural quality. The most desirable Primavera wares are the hand-made artist-decorated ones, although those made in a mould are also collectable.

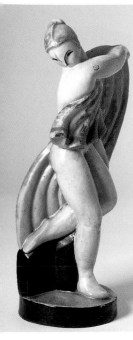

Marks

Hand-made Primavera wares are invariably signed on the base, usually by the potter/modeller and the decorator, and in addition always carry the Primavera mark. Signatures are either hand-painted or are impressed in block capitals. Moulded wares carry an incise-moulded signature.

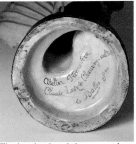

The hand-painted signature, *above*, from the base of the figurine, is that of Claude Levy, one of Primavera's main decorators.
* Other well-known decorators who worked for the design studio, include Colette Gueden and the wife of the director, Charlotte Chaucet-Guillere.

Primavera figures are usually very stylized, as this one *above* is, and often convey a strong sense of movement. The subject is unusual in not having the lithe figure commonly associated with Art Deco ladies. In particular, the legs are somewhat thick and unshapely. Nonetheless, the piece is recognizably of its period, with its stylized face, serpentine-like drape and the contrast between black and mottled ochre.

Condition

The figure above has suffered some damage, notably on the shoulder, knee and drape. Although some blemishes can be disguised, the value is inevitably affected. However, as items that are bought as much for their academic or scarcity value as for their decorative value, the fall in price is not great.

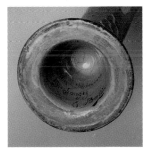

M (for Madeleine) Saugez, whose signature appears on the base of the vase, *above*, was another important Primavera decorator.
* Well-known Primavera designers include Jean Jacques Adnet, René Buthaud (see pp. 66-7), Marcel Renard and Leon Zack.

Glazes

Primavera earthenware tends to have a reddish tone, often with evidence of some gentle crazing, usually apparent from the inside, as is the case with the two pieces shown here. In the 1920s crackled glazes were made in electric kilns and were sometimes used as a ground for painting and other decoration. Those produced for Primavera were made by the Longwy factory and bear that name. Crackle wares were also made by Boch Frères and Royal Copenhagen.

CLARICE CLIFF (1)

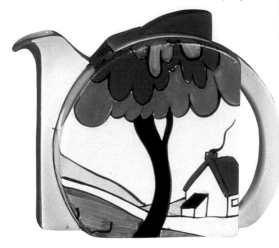

A Clarice Cliff teapot
c.1935; ht 4¹/₂in/11.5cm; value code F

Identification checklist for pottery designed by Clarice Cliff

1. Are motifs bold and decisive?
2. Are colours bright, almost garish?
3. Are landscapes highly stylized?
4. Is there a mark on the base?
5. Is the piece hand-painted?
6. Are enamels laid on thickly, so that brush strokes are visible?
7. Is the shape inventive and almost futuristic?
8. Is there any black outline or banding, either around motifs or rims?

Clarice Cliff (British, 1899-1972)

Clarice Cliff dominated the British pottery scene during the late 1920s and 30s. She joined A. J. Wilkinson's Royal Staffordshire Pottery in Burslem in 1916, where she learned all aspects of pottery-making including modelling, firing, and so on. In 1927 the firm recognized her talent and enthusiasm and set her up in a studio in their nearby Newport Pottery with a team of paintresses. The first pieces were very successful and she became a household name, continuing to produce a wide range of wares until the outbreak of the War.

74

Marks

Most but not all pieces are marked. A variety of different marks was used. Pieces often carry impressed dates, although these may indicate the date of production rather than of design or decoration. The pattern name was often given alongside the Clarice Cliff signature. Pattern names and signatures were initially handwritten; later they were stamped and eventually, were lithographed. Pieces also carry the factory name, which was printed. Marked fakes exist but can usually be identified as such (see pp. 76-7).

* Hand-painted signatures and marks were phased out by c.1931.

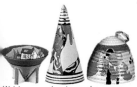

Tablewares dominate the range, among them tea sets, trays, jugs, bowls, baskets, and so on. Cliff also designed book ends, candlesticks, figurines and masks. A distinctive and very extensive range of shapes and patterns were used. Many forms are highly innovative – exemplified by the cone-shaped sugar sifter, beehive honey pot and futuristic bowl *above*, but Cliff also produced more traditional wares that represented an economically safe compromise. Her first successful range, *Bizarre Ware*, was launched in 1928. Other ranges followed soon after, with patterns gradually becoming more elaborate, although Cliff took care to ensure that each design was fully applicable to a full range of shapes and sizes.

Lines were exclusive and were sold in many top department stores. As a result, there were many cheaper imitations on the market.

Identification
The pottery was produced by Wilkinson's at their Newport works in Stoke on Trent. The Newport Pottery pattern books and contemporary advertisements can be used to identify patterns. Sometimes different names were used for the different colours in which patterns appeared.

Glazes
The body of pieces is earthenware, covered in a distinctive "honey glaze", a warm yellow-tinted glaze which gives an ivory colour. Glazing is not rigidly controlled. Enamels are usually laid on relatively thickly so that the brush strokes are visible.

Condition
Check condition carefully. Restoration is not always easy to detect. Look particularly at spouts and handles, and run a finger around rims and bases to check for chipping or repainting. Look out for any slight variation in the colour where the pattern may have been touched up.

Collecting
Cliff pieces are usually collected by pattern or object, rather than in sets. Look for a good balance of form and pattern. *Crocus*, the earliest floral design is the least collectable range because it was so popular at the time and therefore produced in large quantities. Similarly, the more traditional shapes are less desirable. Rare shapes, usually those with unusual rims or flanges caused by warping in the kiln, or those made in several sections joined together, are also desirable. Collectors like the strong geometric forms; floral moulded pieces tend to be ignored, as do the flower vases in water lily form. The rarest range is *Inspiration* (see overleaf), followed by others that use experimental techniques. Cliff's extensive range included many small objects, providing an opportunity for the collector of miniatures or for those with limited space or budget.

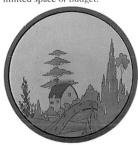

Cliff designed all her own wares, which were then hand-painted, sometimes by a number of people in production-line fashion. The various ranges are named, as are some glaze techniques. Early geometric patterns are regular in design, and employ wide bands of colour. Later patterns are more abstract and use finer banding, sometimes to provide a textured background to floral or landscape motifs. Decoration is sometimes but not always outlined in black. Many wares depict landscapes; these have a lot in common with the work of illustrators and stained glass artists of the period. Many show cottages (especially with a red roof) in country gardens, or a house at the side of a hill, as in the plate *above*. Trees are often drawn with long, spindly trunks surmounted by clouds of foliage.

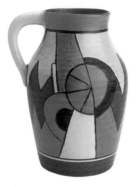 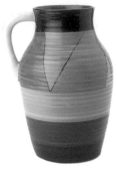

Fakes

Genuine Cliff, *above left*, can usually be distinguished from the many reproductions and fakes on the market, such as that shown *above right*. The standard of painting on the fakes is usually poor and the colour enamels washed out. The honey glaze is often murky, and unevenly applied. The fake shown here is relatively competent but lacks the definition of the genuine piece. Also, the handle is a little thin, and the unglazed footrim somewhat narrow and irregular. This also shares with other fakes the tendency toward pronounced ribbing.

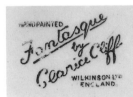 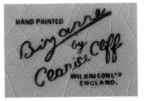

Fake marks

Fakes can also be identified by the marks. On genuine pieces the mark is usually smooth, like the *Fantasque* signature, *above left*. A crackle effect like the one of the faked *Bizarre* signature, *above right*, may be cause for suspicion (although a few genuine pieces have appeared with such crazing).
* On flatware, three circles or stilt marks around the signature where the pot stood in the kiln are a sign of authenticity.
* There are also some genuine reproductions, but these are clearly dated.

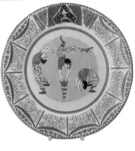

Circus series

This plate, one of a set, was designed c.1934 by Laura Knight as part of her now very collectable *Circus* series for Clarice Cliff (although the series was not a great commercial success in the 30s). The borders and faces are printed, while the rest is hand-painted in stencil, then gilded.
* Other leading Cliff designers included Dod Proctor, and Graham Sutherland, who designed a dinner service decorated with a lively horse motif. Frank Brangwyn designed large circular plaques colourfully decorated with figural subjects (taken from panels originally intended to be hung in the Palace of Westminster).

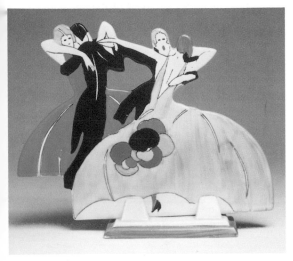

Figures and novelty wares

Age of Jazz figures, like this dancing couple, are much sought after.
These have a three-dimensional effect but are in fact freestanding
plaques.
* Not all novelty items are as highly collectable – for example, Cliff
toby jugs have never been in strong demand.

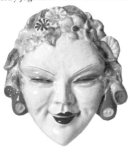

Masks

The series of masks, which
includes wall pockets and some
very desirable wall masks, is very
collectable, geometric types being
the most desirable. Cliff designed
some of these pieces herself;
others bear the incise-cast initials
of the designer. This example is
relatively well modelled, with a
lot of facial creasing: not all
examples have as much. The
moulded floral garland seen here
is popular: other Cliff masks also
tended to feature various types of
floral headdresses.
* In Cliff masks the subject is
shown face-on; on masks by rival
firms they tend to be in profile.

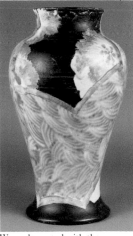

Wares decorated with the
Inspiration design and executed in
the characteristic blue and lilac
colours are particularly sought-
after. This 1930 baluster-shaped
vase, although typical of the
Inspiration range, is a
comparatively rare and thus
particularly desirable piece. It
has a hand-painted Clarice Cliff
signature on the underside of
the base.

SUSIE COOPER

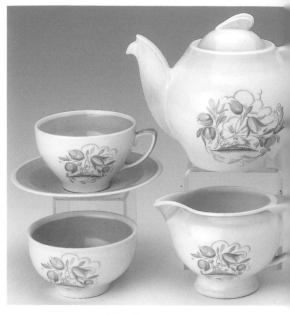

*A Susie Cooper tea set
c.1935; value code F*

Identification checklist for the pottery of Susie Cooper
1. Is the form relatively traditional, possibly rounded, with innovation perhaps confined to any lid or handle?
2. If a tea-set, is it in autumnal shades?
3. Is the piece earthenware?
4. Is it signed? (But see Signatures, *opposite*).
5. Does the decoration have any floral motifs, thick bands of bright colours, or a spotted design?
6. Is the decoration precisely executed, with great attention to detail, and an element of understatement?
7. Does the piece have a robust feel?

Decorative techniques
Susie Cooper used a variety of techniques, including under- and overglazed decoration, and experimented with new methods, such as sgrafitto, crayons, and tube-lining.

Incised stonewares
A series of incised stonewares was produced in the 1930s. Flowers and feathered leaves were preferred, as well as patterns with bright dots, dashes and even exclamation marks. Most tea sets were in autumnal russets and greens.

Collecting Susie Cooper
The most collectable wares are those made before 1939. After the War, bone china replaced earthenware as her favoured material. This is lighter in weight than earthenware and less robust in appearance. Collectors of Susie Cooper will find a catalogue of her wares (see pp. 186-7) very helpful in distinguishing between pre- and post-War designs, especially as many of the designs from the 1920s and 30s have been reproduced since the War.

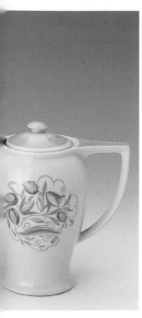

Shapes and patterns

Most Susie Cooper wares have shape and pattern names and numbers. The tea set shown is in the *Kestrel* shape, introduced in 1932, and in production until the 50s. Other shapes of the period were *Curlew* (1932); *Wren* (1934); *Jay* (1935); *Falcon* (1937) and *Spiral* (1938). The pattern is *Dresden Spray*, which has been transfer-printed. It was first used c.1935 and was one of her most popular. Others from the period include *Tadpoles; Scarlet runner beans; Nosegay; Polka dots;* and *Cromer.*
* Patterns were not usually confined to a specific shape but might appear on any number of forms.

Early wares

Susie Cooper worked for A.E. Gray c.1925-1930, decorating a variety of wares in floral, abstract or, more rarely, geometric designs. Some of her early work for Gray has lustre trims or finishes in a variety of colours. Initially, she followed established patterns, but soon was allowed to design her own. To this period belong her wares with solid bands of colours, with as many as five or six colours on one piece. Unlike on similar wares by Clarice Cliff, these thick bands of colour were not isolated, but have a more random, naïve feel. Susie Cooper seldom used overall decoration. Geometric and floral motifs were sometimes combined on one piece. She also did some nursery wares for Gray.

The Susie Cooper Pottery (English, established 1931)

From 1930 Cooper designed and produced her own wares, buying in blanks (undecorated earthenware bases) from other manufacturers. In 1931 she set up her own pottery, the Susie Cooper Pottery, in Burslem, Staffordshire. Designs were generally rather understated, certainly when compared to those of Clarice Cliff (see pp. 74 7). A few had sgraffito decoration, but most were hand-painted.

From the mid-30s some designs were lithographed or transfer-printed, but they nevertheless retained a hand-finished feel. Colours became more subtle in this period. Autumnal shades were particularly preferred. The pottery produced a range of wares, in particular vases, jugs and tea and dinner sets.

Clean, traditional designs were tempered with innovation – for example, tureens often had a self-supporting lid that could be turned upside down and used as a serving dish.

Signatures

Some, but not all, of the Gray wares decorated by Susie Cooper have a printed backstamp and her initials SV (for Vera) C or SC. Cooper's designs for Gray were still used after she left the firm, although not always on the original shapes: the pattern numbers during her period at Gray are those between the late 2000s and the mid-8000s. Numbers not within these figures cannot be Susie Cooper designs.

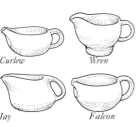

Curlew *Wren*

Jay *Falcon*

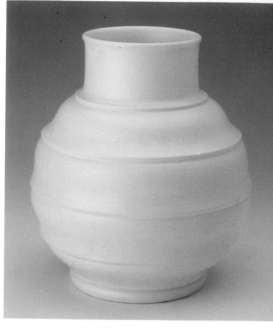

An earthenware vase by Keith Murray
c.1935; ht 10in/25.4cm; value code F

Identification checklist for Keith Murray's ceramics
1. Has the piece a simple geometric form?
2. Is any decoration integral to the form, rather than applied to the surface?
3. Is the glaze semi-matt?
4. Is the piece signed with Murray's full script signature?
5. Is the body earthenware?
6. Is it ribbed?

Keith Murray (New Zealander/British, 1892-1981)
Keith Murray spent most of his working life in England. A trained architect, his background is evident in the architectural, Modernist ceramic wares he produced in the 1930s and 40s. From the late 1930s he also made glass for the Staffordshire firm of Stevens & Williams and was one of the few designers in England to actively promote Modernist principles in his designs.

Murray's work is instantly recognizable for its simple geometric forms and lack of surface embellishment. Decoration and form are nearly always integral. Vases, in which he specialized, are often ribbed and fluted. Many have narrow circular footrims. Murray also produced inkstands, bowls, candlesticks, tablewares, and litho-printed commemorative wares celebrating Edward VIII. His slip wares were introduced after 1936 and continued in production until the mid-1950s. His simple functional designs continued to be popular during the 1940s.

Authenticity

Murray's work, especially his vases and bowls, is much reproduced today. However, these modern wares are not intended to deceive: they have a mass-produced, Constructivist look that distinguishes them from the originals, and they do not bear Murray's signature. The first rule in buying Murray is: if it's not marked, it's not Murray. Fakes, deliberately intended to deceive, have not so far appeared on the market.

Pre-war signatures

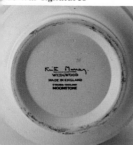

The full script signature like this one, from the underside of the vase shown *opposite* appears on pre-war items.
* Murray's black basalt wares, the rarest of all his products, are signed in red on the base.

Post-war signatures

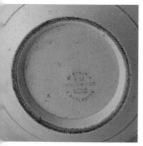

On items made after 1941 the initials "KM" and the Barlaston mark, as shown *above*, are usually used..
* Another difference to note between pre- and post-war wares is that post-1945 wares tend to have a crazed surface, whereas those from the pre-war period invariably have a smooth finish.

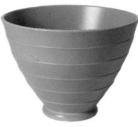

Murray used a distinct range of glazes; these were matt, semi-matt or celadon satin, and were first developed in the Deco period. Some have names – for example, the ivory-white of the vase shown opposite was first used in 1933, and is known as "moonstone". Other preferred colours include matt straw, matt green and matt grey. The blue of the bowl *above* is duck-egg blue, a popular clear pre-war glaze.
* Some 30s glazes continued to be produced after 1940, including green, moonstone and straw.

Tableware for Wedgwood

From 1933 Murray worked part-time for Wedgwood, designing several ranges of hand-thrown and hand-turned tablewares and other functional but ornamental items. His designs for them were in production within a year of the beginning of their association. His first work in 1933 was on the new Annular service, illustrated *below*. This was made in two versions, one with a matt glaze, the other with painted decoration.

Patterns

As well as plain glazes, Murray also designed patterns for tableware. The most popular Murray patterns, designed from 1934, were *Lotus*, *Weeping Willow* (also known as *Green Tree*), *Iris*, *Pink Flower*, and *Pink and Red Flower*, as well as the border patterns *Lotus* and *Radio*.

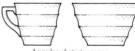

Annular *shape tea wares*

iris
pattern

green tree
pattern

lotus
pattern

JOSIAH WEDGWOOD & SONS

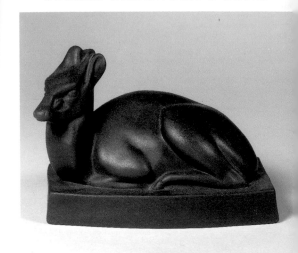

*A Wedgwood seated deer by John Skeaping for Wedgwood
c.1935; ht 4¹/₂in/11cm; value code F*

Identification checklist for the ceramics designed by
John Skeaping for Wedgwood
1. Is the piece an animal or bird?
2. If an animal, is it in a passive stance?
3. Does the piece have a reflective matt or semi-matt
glaze in cream, celadon green moonstone or black
basalt?
4. Is the J.Skeaping mark incise-cast into the side
of the piece, together with the impressed Wedgwood
mark?
5. If a figure, is the area underneath it filled in, and
possibly decorated – for example, with formalized
shrubbery?

Note
Apart from the work done by Keith Murray (see pp. 78-9), the most
significant contribution to Wedgwood Art Deco design was the work of
John Skeaping.

John Rattenbury Skeaping
Skeaping was employed as a
designer by Wedgwood from
1926. He specialized in animals,
and also made some birds, and his
work influenced many lesser
potters of the period. Of the 14
designs he created for Wedgwood,
10 were in production through the
30s. They were somewhat
reminiscent of the work of George
Sandoz (see p. 123).
* Animals were usually produced
82

first in basalt and then in a variety
of colours and glazes - for
example, the seal is often found
in tan or celadon green.

Note
A number of Skeaping pieces
have fitted wooden stands. If the
object is a very tight fit the stand
should be professionally removed,
because the figures are prone to
cracking as the wood tightens
with age.

Other ceramic animals

With the notable exception of a bull designed by Arnold Machin printed with zodiac signs by Ravilious (see *below*), most Wedgwood animals of this period are by Skeaping. Similar wares were retailed by Primavera (see pp. 70-1). Royal Lancastrian also produced animal figures (including bears, sea lions, and a gazelle). Staffordshire produced the very popular "sylvac bunnies".

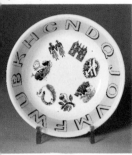

The attractive utility wares designed by Eric Ravilious for Wedgwood during the late 1930s are currently very popular with collectors. Prices have risen accordingly and even damaged items such as the *Alphabet* plate *above*, which is slightly chipped, are collectable, although they fetch around half the price of perfect pieces. Ravilious designed the *Alphabet* nurseryware in 1937; the decoration was transfer-printed, usually in straightforward bands used for pastel colours. Pink, yellow and grey predominate. The shapes tended to be those used for the firm's standard current tableware.
* Other currently sought-after Ravilious designs are the boat-race chalice, a zodiac series and a lemonade set decorated with garden implements. The pieces are still quite widely available and include whole dinner services.
* Most Ravilious designs were not executed until the 1950s. Some were reissued in 1987 in response to the recent increase in public demand. These lack the characteristic signs of wear of the originals.

Ravilious marks

Ravilious wares are signed in a small rectangular panel "designed by Eric Ravilious" and carry an imprinted Wedgwood mark.

Josiah Wedgwood & Sons (British, founded 1759)

During the Art Deco period Wedgwood produced both traditional and avant-garde designs. As well as the leading designers, Murray and Skeaping, other Wedgwood designers of the period were:
* Norman Wilson (who experimented with glaze effects)
* Victor Skellern
* Millicent Taplin
* Alfred and Louise Powell, best known for lustre decoration
* Anna Katrina Zinkeisen
* Erling B. Olsen.

Wedgwood marks

In the 20s and 30s the impressed mark "Wedgwood, made in England," was used. The printed Portland vase mark on bone china dates from 1878 and continued to be used, in a slightly different form, in the 1920s and 30s. After the 1940s the Barlaston mark (see pp. 81) was introduced on creamwares.

Wedgwood Fairyland wares (see below) are identified by the letter Z and a pattern number on the base. Some of the rarer examples of Daisy Makeig-Jones's work, such as rectangular plaques, bear her signature, usually in gilt, and often hidden among the decoration.

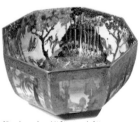

During the 1920s and 30s Wedgwood produced a range of lustre wares, including *Chinese* and *Butterfly* lustre and the *Fairyland* series, shown *above*, which is the most popular and expensive type. The imagery of pixies and goblins is not usually associated with the Art Deco period and in fact harks back more to the fairytale world of 1900, but the shapes and bright colours of these wares are comparatively "modern" and made them popular in the 20s and 30s. These wares were emulated by Carlton (see p. 91).

SHELLEY

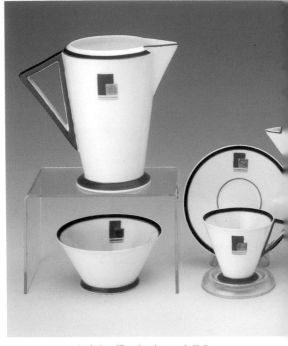

A selection of Eve-*shaped teaware by Shelley c.1932, ht of teapot 10in/25.4cm; value code F*

Identification checklist for Shelley pottery
1. Do rims have silver lustre or coloured banding?
2. Is the piece signed?
3. Are wares with geometric designs of good quality bone china?
4. Do handles have innovative forms?
5. Is use made of the underlying ground in all-over decoration?

Shelley (British, 1872-1966)
The factory, originally known as Wileman & Co., and later trading under the name "Foley", changed its name to Shelley in 1925, although the Shelley stamp had been used as early as 1910. During the 20s and 30s the firm tempered the more avant-garde lines with commercially safe classic shapes and designs. A large number of tea and dinner sets were made; complete sets are at a premium, especially those designed by Mabel Lucie Attwell. No fakes are known, although there are many contemporary lookalikes, as the firm set a

standard for porcelain in the 20s and 30s.

Decoration
Designs were hand-painted in enamels and had a transfer-printed outline. Trees, flowers and the sun were popular motifs, and geometric designs were often used. Striking colour combinations include yellow and black, and mauve and green. Wares in jade green combined with a silver lustre trim are especially desirable. Colours became progressively more subdued and florals less stylized during the 1930s.

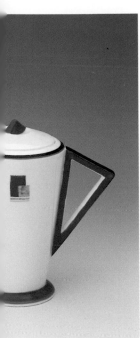

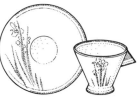

Mode shape
Blue Iris pattern

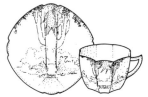

Queen Anne shape
Sunrise and Tall Trees pattern

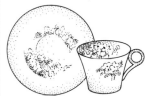

Regent shape
Yellow Phlox pattern

Collecting

Not all Shelley wares are sought after by collectors, but those from the Deco period are very desirable, in particular the shape named *Eve*, shown *above*, which combines an innovative design with practicality or fitness for purpose. The pure decoration, clean overlapping geometrics and iron-red and black trim are also typical of the best Shelley. The most successful designs are simple. Some of the more innovative ones proved impracticable – for example, *Vogue* and *Mode* had solid handles which were difficult to use, and these were not in production for very long.

Marks

All genuine Shelley wares are marked. A script signature inside a cartouche is the most common. Anything marked "Fine Bone China" is post-1945. Pattern numbers progressed from around 11,000 in the mid-20s to around 13,000 in 1939. The serial number for seconds begins with a 2.

Nursery wares

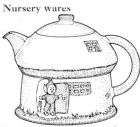

This highly successful area for Shelley used the talents of two illustrators, Mabel Lucie Attwell, who joined the firm in 1926, and Hilda Cowham, who was taken on in 1928. They designed a range of nursery, or children's wares, with unusual shapes, including a toadstool teapot, *above*, and story-book type illustrations. Some wares were decorated with characters and events from Attwell's own stories. In the 1930s Attwell also designed an animal tea set and and some figurines of fairies and other characters. Nursery waves are still popular today.

POOLE POTTERY

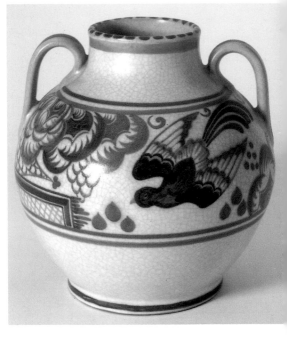

*A Poole Pottery polychrome earthenware vase
c.1930; ht approx 9in/23cm; value code F*

Identification checklist for Poole polychrome pottery
1. Does the piece use a distinctive palette, perhaps with blue as the dominant colour?
2. Is the decoration stylized, possibly with floral motifs?
3. Does the piece have a semi-matt glaze?
4. Is there an impressed Carter-Stabler-Adams mark and a painter's signature or mark?
5. Is the body red clay with an overlying grey-white glaze?

Carter, Stabler and Adams (British, established 1873)
This firm, which operated from the Poole Pottery in Dorset, was established as Carter and Co. In 1921 it expanded and took the combined surnames of its partners Charles Carter, Harold and Phoebe Stabler and John Adams. The firm was an unusual and successful hybrid of an art and a commercial pottery, although it became increasingly commercial throughout the 1930s.

In the 1920s the pottery specialized in small, decorative, functional wares, such as vases, biscuit barrels, preserve jars and ashtrays. It also made a number of portrait plates depicting stylish faces, and a series of ship plates.
* Although it was not officially known by this name until 1963, the firm's early wares are sometimes known as, and described in auction house catalogues as, Poole.

Tablewares

Small morning tea and coffee sets were produced during the 1920s, but these were decorative rather than utilitarian. Tableware shapes began to be introduced in larger ranges in 1933, but were still not produced in any quantity and remained exclusive. It was not until 1936 that the first competitive standard machine-made tableware, *Streamline*, was produced.

Patterns

Pieces are collected by design rather than by artist. Collectable ranges produced by the pottery during the 1930s include the following:
* 1933 *Studland*, a plain body with elaborate and angular handles, either in dark green, or blue with a mottled finish, or painted with modern leaf and floral patterns
* c.1933 *Picotee*, rounded shapes, and Everest, ribbed, with solid diamond-shaped handles, both decorated in plain glaze colours
* 1936 *Streamline*, simplified traditional shapes, with combinations of two-colour glazes in subdued autumnal colours, known after 1945 as *Twintone*. Some wares were decorated with small floral motifs.

Marks

The firm used a variety of marks: if the base is unmarked, the piece is almost certainly not Poole. Usually the base is impressed "Carter, Stabler, Adams Ltd" or "C.S.A.", and includes the decorator's monogram. Some pieces have pattern codes – which are usually two-letters. If three letters are shown, the third usually indicates the dominant colour. Few pieces are dated: those that are may have been made as commemorative pieces for specific organizations. Later examples, after 1963, carry just the Poole mark. No fakes have been identified.

Hand-thrown or moulded?

Hand-thrown pieces have irregular ribbing on the inside and a less clinical appearance than is usual with moulded wares.

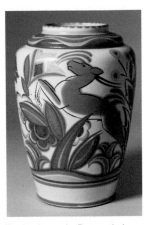

Production at the Pottery during the 1920s and early 30s consisted largely of hand-thrown ornamental stonewares, such as this vase, *above*. There are some plain, white-glazed and two-tone wares, but the Pottery is particularly associated with floral and bird patterns, usually in harmonious blends of deep, subtle colours under a matt glaze.
* Many Poole wares have a characteristic dentil rim or trim, usually in a colour that repeats one of those used in the decoration (– for example, see the vase in the main picture).

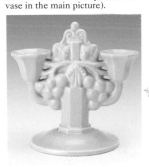

Far more intricate forms can be created using the slipcast method, which gives smooth surfaces and regular shapes, such as on this distinctively shaped candlestick, *above*. Slipcast wares are made by pouring slip (clay mixed with water) into a plaster mould. The plaster absorbs the water and the "cheese hard" clay that forms can then be removed. Mould lines are sometimes distinguishable.

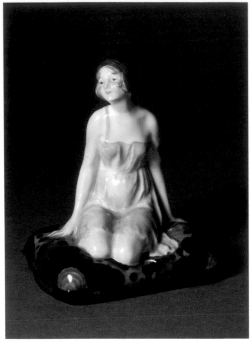

Bone china figure entitled Négligé, *by Lesley Harradine for Doulton c.1927; ht 4³/₄in/12cm; value code F*

Identification checklist for Doulton ceramics
1. Is the piece marked? (See facing page.)
2. Is it bone china?
3. Is the decoration hand-painted?
4. Is the subject a realistic "modern" women?
5. Does the figure have an "English rose" type of face (youthful, with fair colouring, a healthy-looking rounded face and rosy cheeks)?
6. Is the subject shown in a casual pose or situation?
7. Does the piece have a high-gloss glaze?
8. Where the figure is clothed, or partly clothed, are pale flesh tones set against vivid colours, whether bright primaries or pastels?
9. Does the piece convey a mood of joyous abandon and escapism?

Doulton figurines

These formed the staple output of decorative waves during the 20s and 30s. They represent a departure from the Victorian-style crinolined ladies, and the nymphs and sirens so beloved in the Art Nouveau period. Produced primarily for the British market, most have a characteristic "English rose" look.

During the 1930s Beswick produced some figurines which were not particularly popular. Those made by Wade are not nearly as collectable today.

Condition

The exposed limbs of figurines are especially susceptible to being chipped or broken and are therefore the parts most likely to have been restored: look for very subtle changes in skin tones and surface glazes, where retouching may have occurred. Enamels, particularly the blacks, were prone to flaking, and should be examined for signs of overpainting.

The bases, which were mass-produced, sometimes show stress cracks. This need not unduly trouble the prospective purchaser as long as they don't extend more than an inch (2.5cm) from the hole underneath the base or extend to the visible areas of the piece.

Figures were often mounted on table lamp bases; these bases are not especially desirable and may be removed. However, this should always be done professionally, as the rubber retainer has a tendency to vulcanize and explode on contact.

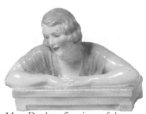

Most Doulton figurines of the period are depicted full length; head and shoulder busts, like this one, *above*, are relatively uncommon, although it is characteristic of Doulton in other respects. The casual pose is especially typical: Doulton ladies are also shown reclining on sofas, and in other informal situations – a style of sculpture that would have been considered avant-garde in its day (see also p. 23).

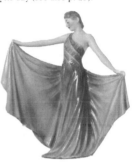

Most of the subjects are shown in the context of their new-found freedom. This is often reflected by the costumes – for example, elegant evening gowns such as the one shown *above*, or négligés, or the dress of a gala ball poppet. Others wear carnival costume, which is particularly evocative of the 1920s.

Marks

The figures are usually painted on the base with the words "Potted by Royal Doulton", and those from the 1920s and 30s have a hand-painted title (as opposed to the printed mark used in the post-war period). They also carry an "HN" number – the factory reference number which gives the title and records when the piece was introduced and when it was withdrawn. Reprints of contemporary Doulton catalogues are available and these provide valuable information on individual items.

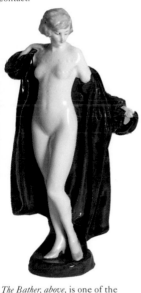

The Bather, above, is one of the most famous figures of the period; as well as this nude, risqué version, there was also a more modest one, clothed in a black painted swimsuit.
* Doulton figurines are often clothed in costumes of one bold principal colour.

CARLTON

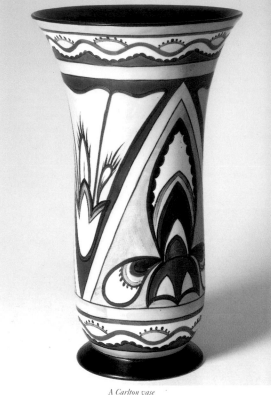

A Carlton vase
c.1930; ht 10in/25.4cm; value code F

Identification checklist for Carlton ceramics
1. Is the piece signed "Carlton ware" in script?
2. Is the decoration hand-painted?
3. Is the shape inventive, and perhaps futuristic?
4. Is a dramatic effect achieved through the juxtaposition of bright colours?
5. Is the design geometric, perhaps with formalized flower heads or brocade-type motifs?
6. If the piece is a vase, is it less than 12in (30cm) tall, and if a bowl, is it less than that in diameter?
7. Is there a semi-matt glaze?

Carlton (British, 1890-1957)
Carlton ware was produced by the Carlton Works at Stoke, between 1890 and 1957, the pottery division of Wiltshaw and Robinson. It was renamed Carltonware Ltd in 1958.

Marks
Individual designers are not identified; pieces carry the words "Carlton ware" in script. Some bear the patent word "AUST", to indicate that it was legal to sell them in Australia.

Types of ware

Ceramics produced by Carlton during the 1920s and 30s fall into three distinct categories:
* geometric design work, exemplified by the vase shown
* exotically coloured lustre art pottery.
* moulded tableware and small, useful novelty items such as dishes in the form of leaves.

Carlton was one of the first companies to produce oven-to-table wares: these were heat-resistant whitewares with a wavy-lined border in three colours. They have yet to become popular with collectors.

Shapes and decoration

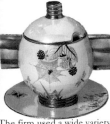

The firm used a wide variety of forms, including some very popular inventive Modernist shapes, such as that of the covered bowl *above*. However, at the same time they also continued to produce their more traditional items. Colours tend to be bright (as in the vase, *opposite*). From c.1935 softer tones and pastels were used in preference to bolder shades. Some pieces incorporate silver lustre for a dramatic effect, sometimes in the form of a lightning motif. The decoration is hand-painted, often featuring stylized flowers.

Collecting

Prices for Carlton's lustre range have increased dramatically in recent years, although they are still lower than for the lustre wares of their closest rival, Wedgwood. Very much the rarest, as well as the best and thus the most collectable, of the Carlton pieces, are the geometric designs exemplified by the vase illustrated, followed by the chinoiserie-style lustre pieces.

The more mundane leaf-moulded items, which accounted for most of Carlton's output in the 1920s and 30s, were made in greater numbers and are less collectable.

Lustre wares

Carlton's lustre wares were produced in the wake of Wedgwood's success with this type of effect. The technique involved the controlled use of an iridescent, high-gloss, pearlized glaze, which gave pieces a richly coloured, jewel-like appearance. Irregularities that occurred during firing were often masked by the gilt detail which was applied freehand afterwards. Carlton lustre is generally on a cobalt blue ground (also a Wedgwood characteristic), sometimes allied with a mottled tangerine-coloured matt glaze. Decorative features include butterflies, chinoiserie and naturalistic flora. Carlton used as many as twelve colours for their lustre ware, many of them dark.
* The lustre wares produced by the firm of Maling in Newcastle upon Tyne have now become highly collectable. These pieces have conventional, underglaze printed and enamelled floral decoration with an iridescent surface glaze.

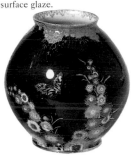

Among Carlton's lustre wares was a range that depicted fairy gardens and magical landscapes, and was perhaps inspired by Wedgwood's highly successful *Fairyland* range. The vase *above* is typical: the design, which is bright and delicate, is hand-enamelled on a printed outline; the enamels, which are applied over the glaze, are slightly raised. The interiors of these pieces have a slightly iridescent, pearlized effect not found on Wedgwood *Fairyland*.
* Wedgwood *Fairyland* employs underglaze (as opposed to overglaze) enamels, resulting in a smooth surface, rather than a raised one (see p. 83). The Wedgwood lustre wares continue to be more desirable to collectors than Carlton lustre ware.

LENCI

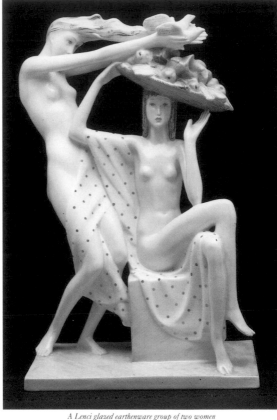

A Lenci glazed earthenware group of two women
c.1937; ht 20in/49.25cm; value code C

Identification checklist for Lenci ceramics
1. Is the subject female?
2. Are the figures idealized?
3. Do the women have either serene, or coy, coquettish expressions?
4. Is the decoration hand-painted?
5. Is there a smooth semi-matt finish in white or flesh tones?
6. Is the figure wearing a hat, possibly depicted as straw?
7. Are the painted eyebrows exaggerated?

Lenci Workshops (Italian, estabd 1919)
The Lenci workshops in Turin produced a mixture of stylish and kitsch glazed earthenware and porcelain figures. Most are single subjects; groups such as the one, *above*, are less common. Lenci also made a number of wall masks, and in the 1930s produced a series of highly colourful caricatures.

Glazes

A feature of Lenci figures is the use of combined glazes on a single piece – for example, many have matt subjects on a shiny gloss base.

Marks

Lenci figures sometimes come with paper labels identifying the factory; individual designers usually remained anonymous. There are various marks for the Lenci workshops. Sometimes the single word "Lenci" is painted on the figure. Alternatively, the mark "Lenci Made in Italy Torino" may be found.

Collectors should note that on some signed pieces, the word Lenci reads backwards – the result of having been set in positive rather then reverse in the mould.

Recognition points

* Hair is often very blond, almost impossibly yellow as in the two figures on this page.
* Hats, especially straw ones, feature prominently and may be highly exaggerated as in the cornucopia of fruit worn by the woman in the main picture.

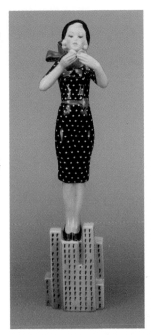

The imagery of some Lenci figures is emphatically that of the 1920s or 30s, such as this lady in polka dot dress standing on high-rise apartment blocks while powdering her nose.
* Not all Lenci figures have recognizably period features, although even those that do not, display a combination of naïveté and sophistication that is characteristic of the period.

Collecting

Some of the less successful Lenci figures, including some nudes, border on the kitsch. These are generally less sought-after by collectors than the more sophisticated pieces and those that depict contemporary figures or situations.

Royal Dux

The Royal Dux factory in Bohemia produced some figures that were similar to those made by Lenci: they used matt glazes and depicted lean, leggy women, often nudes. These figures tend to have more in common with the stylized creations which are usually associated with the 1920s and 30s.

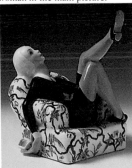

Many Lenci figures are very modern for their period: to show a langorous woman reclining in an armchair would have been highly innovative. Typically for Lenci women who are clothed, this figure is depicted in relatively chic, accurate contemporary dress.
* Lenci occasionally took some artistic license with their portrayal of the human form – note the impossible length of the girl's arms, and the blue star-spangled hair of the woman in the main picture.

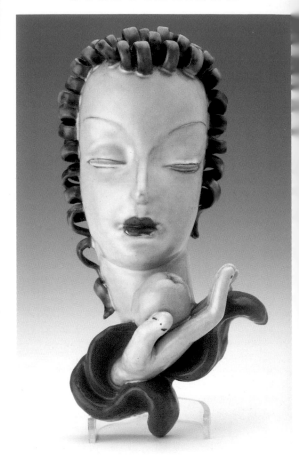

A polychrome wall mask by Goldscheider
c.1930; ht 13¹/₂in/34.5cm; value code F

Identification checklist for Goldscheider ceramics
1. Is the costume exotic?
2. Are the colours rich and boldly contrasted?
3. Is any hair, especially of wall masks, in ringlets and glazed in bright colours?
4. If a mask, is it terracotta and partly hollowed at the back?
5. Is the piece marked?
6. If figures are included, are they very stylized?
7. Are eyes narrow, perhaps half-closed or downcast?
8. If earthenware, is it cream-coloured with vivid underglaze?

Goldscheider (Austrian, 1885-1953)

The firm made figures, wall masks and large earthenware sculptures and during the 1920s and 30s also produced plaster and ceramic versions of the bronzes of Lorenzl, Zach and other major sculptors. Some pieces were made for export to the United States.

Figures

In the early 1920s the most popular pieces were lithe, somewhat idealized figures mostly in period attire, often a couple dancing.

Masks

Wall masks, popular in the Art Deco period, were made by several companies, including many based in Staffordshire, but those by Goldscheider are considered more desirable. The firm made a series of six or more designs, all of the same size; these are hand-painted, and have a sculpted look. Serene, stylized facial expressions are coupled with bright colours, typically using lots of iron red and yellow. The range also included a few Negro studies.

Condition

The soft terracotta from which the masks are made is prone to chipping, and paint can also wear: check that it has not been retouched. The back plate should carry the transfer-printed mark.

Marks

Pieces after 1918 have a transfer-printed mark, "Goldscheider Wien. Made in Austria", which superseded the earlier, pre-war mark of an embossed rectangular pad of a kneeling figure from Greek pottery. Commissioned wares sometimes carry the name of the designer as well, and a serial number. A few are still found with their original paper label.

Staffordshire Goldscheider

In the late 1930s the rights to produce Goldscheider figures were taken up by the Staffordshire company Myott, Son & Co. Ltd, whose versions were marked "Goldscheider made in England". These are not as sought-after as the Austrian versions. Goldscheider set up its own British pottery in 1946, and pieces from this period have a signature mark.

ROSENTHAL (Bauaria, 1879-present)

Other collectable, fine-quality ceramic figures were produced by the art department of this factory, who also made tableware porcelain, and were noted for their responsiveness to contemporary tastes.

Rosenthal pieces use inventive shapes and tend to be ornate in form or pattern.

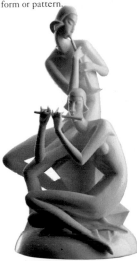

Rosenthal figures have an individual, sculptural quality – seen clearly in this piece from 1927 – which gradually became more stylized through the 1920s and 30s. Dancers were also depicted, often wearing colourful, exotic or futuristic costumes.
* Rosenthal also produced a range of cabinet objects, including animals and stylized figures modelled in white.

Collecting

Rosenthal work is relatively underrated: it is probably the nearest equivalent to work by Meissen, but is far more affordable. The figures are more desirable than the tablewares, which are not really worth collecting at all, unless decorated or designed by a leading artist.

Marks

Pieces are incise-marked with the designer's name on the side of the base, and have printed green crossed roses and crown marks underneath.

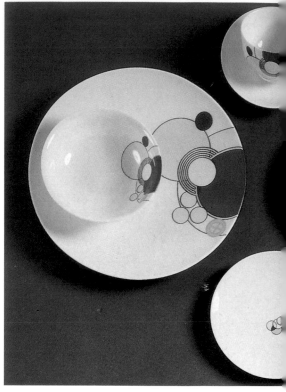

A six-piece porcelain place setting designed by Frank Lloyd Wright for Noritake 1922; value code C

Identification checklist for Noritake porcelain
1. Is the pattern modernistic - for example, geometric or cubist, and outlined in black?
2. Is the design rendered in vivid colours?
3. Is the decoration hand-painted?
4. Is there a mark on the base?
5. Is the ground, where not covered by decoration, of fine white porcelain, relatively free of imperfections?
6. Does the piece have a simple, classical shape?
7. Does the piece have a glossy surface?

Noritake (Japan/The United States, established 1904)
Noritake produced hand-painted porcelain on a scale that could compete with printed designs. From 1914 they made mostly tea and dinner wares, matching accessories and novelty pieces and figures.

The American market
During the 1920s and 30s the design team was based in New York. The designs were produced in Japan and reimported to the United States, which was the major market for their more adventurous, and now most collectable designs.

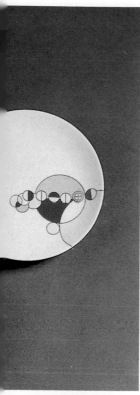

The European market

In addition to those pieces made for the American market, some wares were designed with the British market in mind. These include hand-painted designs of Arab encampments, still fairly readily available in Britain, and French-type tea and decorative wares reminiscent of 18thC styles. The wares made for Europe are often lavish, and many include gilt decoration.

Marks

Wares are marked on the base, usually with the words "Noritake" and "MADE IN JAPAN". The company is still in existence today. Pieces are not dated, so collectors should try to check the date of the design and of the issue of the wares with contemporary catalogues or specialist books: many early designs, including that of the place setting illustrated, remained in production until the 1960s, and may bear later marks,

including "Noritake Nippon Tokikaisha Japan". Documentary information exists on the work of some of the most important designers. The trademark has undergone many changes since 1904 and collectors should also try to familiarize themselves with the appropriate marks for the period.
* Particular attention should be paid to the 1933 mark, which forms the basis of the stamp used by the firm today.
* The "rose china" mark was used in 1946 in preference to the Noritake mark, as wares did not revert to the high pre-war standards until 1947.

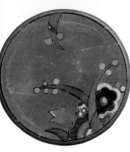

This 1930s plate with a stylized floral design is typical of the more dynamic, diverse and exuberant patterns produced by the firm in this decade.
* Noritake executed wares by a number of top designers, including Frank Lloyd Wright, who designed the place setting shown *opposite*.

Copies

Copies of Noritake wares are known to exist, but usually of the less adventurous stock designs. These were executed by smaller Japanese factories for export, mostly to Europe, and bear a variety of marks on the base, such as "Nippon" and "Samurai".

COWAN POTTERY

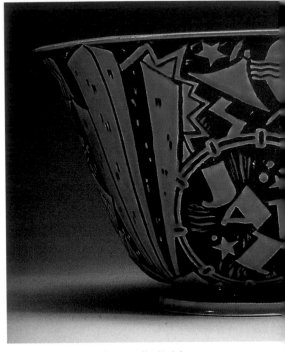

A Cowan Pottery punchbowl in the Jazz pattern
c.1930; ht 8in/20cm; value code C

Identification checklist for Cowan Pottery wares

1. Is the piece marked?
2. Is any painted decoration applied by hand and highly stylized, with a minimal use of colour?
3. Are glazes well applied?
4. Is the modelling of figural work well executed?
5. If earthenware, is the body pale buff in colour?
6. If porcelain, is the body white?
7. If a statuette, is it slipcast, with a hollow body?

Cowan Pottery (American, 1913-31)
This works was founded by Reginald Guy Cowan. The principal wares were decorative vases and figurines. Most early designs were by Cowan himself. In 1927 the works expanded to include the Cowan Pottery Studio Inc. and over the next four years it produced its most impressive and advanced designs, employing outside designers, including Waylande Gregory, Edward and

Thelma Frazier Winter and Paul Manship. The "studio" lines issued in limited editions are highly collectable.

Style
Holloware, statuettes and other items are slipcast and usually glazed in monochrome, although polychrome statuettes in a bright, unnaturalistic palette are found. Statuettes are typically quite large, but, being slipcast, are lightweight.

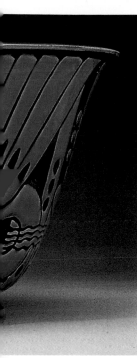

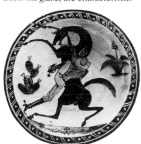

WILHELM HUNT DIEDERICH (The United States, 1884-1953)

Another craftsman working in a consciously modern American style was Hungarian-born Diederich, who emigrated to the United States in 1899. His work includes graphic and textile designs, although he is best known for his metalwork (mostly wrought iron), especially chandeliers with animal motifs. He travelled extensively and developed an interest in ceramics following a trip to North Africa in 1923. For the next decade he produced decorative earthenware in a unique style. Between 1923 and c.1925 all the pieces were individually hand-painted; from the mid-20s many were designed for mass production. Examples of both types are relatively rare today. The earthenware he designed and made in his studio in Woodstock (New York), has a rustic flavour comparable to the tin-glazed provincial pottery of southern Europe. Large dishes, thickly potted in redware and glazed and decorated with earth tones, sometimes on a ground of white tin glaze, are characteristic.

The *Jazz* bowl

Viktor Schreckengost specialized in ceramic decoration in a sophisticated modern style of uniquely American taste. Some of his work was produced by the Cowan Pottery, and his best-known design is probably the *Jazz* punchbowl, *above*. This was designed in 1930, and made in an edition of 50, each slightly different. The bowl and other wares in this pattern are decorated using the sgraffito technique, with images symbolic of the jazz age in New York.

Marks

Pieces designed by Guy Cowan himself are typically marked with the name "Cowan" moulded in relief, sometimes with a monogram "R G" below. Most Cowan products bear impressed, relief-moulded or printed marks, sometimes including the artist's name or monogram. The word "Lakeware" is impressed on some inexpensively produced flower vases (made for florists) between 1927 and 1931.

Many of Diederich's ceramic wares feature equestrian motifs or other figural designs, including greyhounds, ibex, antelope and bulls, depicted in an unmistakeable, lively style, seen in this earthenware platter, c.1929, decorated with the image of a cowboy mounting a horse. The horse is a characteristically lean-legged, long-necked, almost cartoon-like interpretation. The image evokes the American Southwest, where Diederich spent much of his time.

* Some examples include the artist's painted name or initials on the front or underside, but many are unmarked.

MINOR CERAMICS

There are many attractive tablewares in period colours and patterns, available today relatively inexpensively because they are unmarked, not by major craftsmen or not quite as finely executed as the wares shown on the previous pages. There are also a number of novelty items on the market. Perhaps the most popular of these was the tea service in the form of a thatched cottage. In recent years teapots from these ranges have been very eagerly collected. Other novelty pieces include teapots in the form of racing cars, usually bearing the registration plate "T42 OK", and aeroplanes.

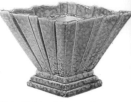

This dish is of the popular sunburst form decorated with a mottled focculated, or random, glaze. It retains its original lozenge-shaped liner. However, it lacks delicacy and the colour has not been controlled with complete success.

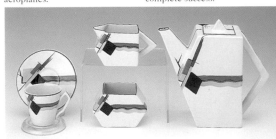

A large number of factories, some of which survived for only a few months, made tea sets of this kind for the masses, especially during the 1930s. Pedigree is usually determined by the type of glaze, the shape and the way the decoration complements the shape. This hand-painted set borrows from the work of major designers, but misinterprets the style: the design is a little heavy in form and is not equally successful on each piece (unlike designs by Clarice Cliff which work in many different scales). The earthenware body is of a similar quality to that of more expensive pieces.

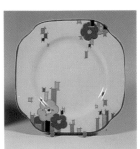
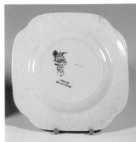

The orange, iron red, black, and yellow used on this plate are all typical of the period, as is the abstract decoration. Pieces like this were made inexpensively by combining mass-produced blanks with mass-produced patterns.
* Most ceramics of the period are signed, as this plate is, but the signature or factory mark is by no means a guarantee of quality or value.

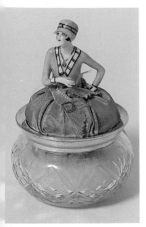

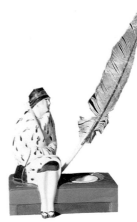

Dressing table wares with figural tops were popular in the 1920s and 30s. There are many types, varying in size from $1/2$in (1.2cm) to around 4in (10cm). This unmarked porcelain powder puff is probably German or Austrian. Any contemporary-looking figure in porcelain is worth looking at as they command a premium. The subject here is unusual: most are either Louis XV Pompadour types with bouffant hair, or naked wanton women. The piece retains its original powder base, a nice but not essential feature – most collectors are interested in the porcelain top, which must be in good condition. Figures are hollow, and pierced to enable the powder puff to be attached.

This nicely modelled, attractive piece is an example of a 1930s type of ware not often found today: porcelain inkstands tend to be vulnerable, and are easily damaged. This example shows late 1930s dress, with short beads and hemline.

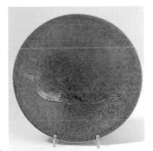

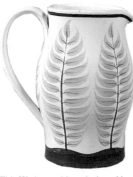

This Wedgwood jug, designed by Alfred and Louise Powell, is attractive, but the modern decoration is compromised by its traditional 18thC form.

This Scandinavian plate is an example of Argenta ware, which uses electrolysis to build silver on stoneware. Argenta ware has gained in popularity in the last five or six years, but is still relatively inexpensive. The Danish makers, Bing & Gröndahl, produced other items in simple, tasteful shapes such as vases with upright rectangular panel forms, sometimes with small shoulder handles. Form and decoration are invariably well balanced, and pieces are hand finished, always against the same mottled jade green semi-matt glaze.
* Silver deposit on tablewares was also used by Lennox in New York, but with more traditional forms and decoration.

SCULPTURE

By the beginning of the 20thC, sculpture had become a very expensive art form beyond the means of most people. Spelter figures, introduced in an attempt to undersell more expensive bronze examples, served only to debase commercial sculpture. The Art Deco years saw the rebirth of sculpture, especially in bronze, as an art form for the masses. Before the First World War pieces were produced as one-off art objects, but the introduction in the late 1920s of mass-production techniques allowed larger quantities to be made and sold. France was the main centre of production, followed by Germany and Austria. German figures tend toward athletic, futuristic types; French work is more evocative of the frivolous side of the jazz age.

Women are the most common subject. They are often athletic or amazonian, as in the work of Marcel Bouraine (see pp. 110-11). Futuristic and theatrical elements, exemplified by the work of Dimitri Chiparus (see pp. 106-7), are common, and figures are often shown performing modern activities, such as smoking. Erotic subjects, such as those of Bruno Zach (see pp. 116-7), are especially collectable; historical figures are less keenly sought after. Sporting subjects are popular, as are pierrots and pierrettes. Children as subjects also made a revival during this period.

Exotic animals, especially those of a sleek and speedy nature, were often featured. Several French sculptors made sea and other birds with a novelty element in the design – for example, a bird in flight would be supported by the tip of a wave. Panthers, gazelles and deer were common, often pursued by Diana-type figures.

The main materials were bronze, and chryselephantine – a novel combination of bronze and ivory popularized in the 1920s. Figures in this medium tend to be more sought-after than pieces entirely in either ivory or bronze, and therefore command a premium. The more ivory used, the more expensive the piece is overall.

Many sculptures were subjected to metallic patination. Gilt and silvered patination were the most favoured, and green was the most popular coloured variety.

Bases acquired a greater degree of importance than before. Green Brazilian onyx, black slate and cream striated marble were the most popular materials.

Figures are usually signed, but not every signed piece is genuine: because of the enormous popularity of Art Deco sculptures, there are many fakes on the market. Period simulated chryselephantine pieces, which are bronzed spelter combined with plastic (often referred to as "ivorene"), can be difficult to identify as the bronze patination can be quite thick. Look underneath and scratch the figure from the inside to check the colour of the metal, which will be yellow if it is genuine bronze, silver if spelter. The development of a technique for graining ivorene faces to resemble ivory makes

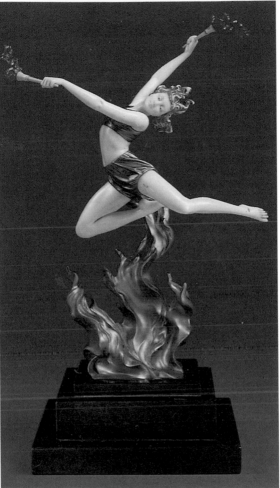

The Flame Leaper, *a cold-painted bronze, ivory and amber figure of an acrobat by Ferdinand Preiss (see pp. 104-5).*

modern copies harder to identify. Look carefully at the finish: there should be no mould lines. Also check how snug and neat the fit is: ivory has a sharp edge and joins flush with any bronze, while ivorene, which is moulded, tends to chamfer on the corners. Fakes are usually applied to very heavy bases, often of marble, to make the overall piece seem heavier and therefore more authentic.

Genuine sculptures will show signs of natural wear, but many bronze figures have been artificially aged by applying salt to the nuts holding the piece to the base, giving the appearance of rust. Genuine pieces will be neither over-bright nor too rusty.

FERDINAND PREISS

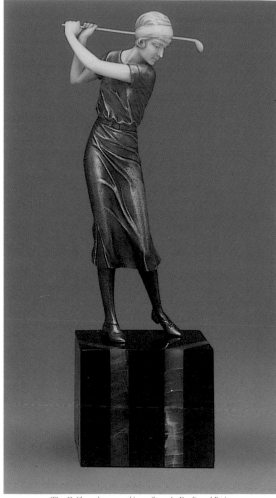

The Golfer, *a bronze and ivory figure by Ferdinand Preiss*
1930s; ht 12^{1}/$_{2}$in/32cm; value code C

Identification checklist for Preiss sculptures
1. Is the figure anatomically correct?
2. Does it bear the "PK" monogram and a signature?
3. Is the face naturalistic, and perhaps tinted to suggest – for example, rouge?
4. Do the costumes have a metallic finish?

Identification point
Most Preiss bases are made of green, black (or a combination of green and black) Brazilian onyx, sometimes banded with black Belgian slate.

Ferdinand Preiss (German, 1882-1943)

Most Preiss figures are made of chryselephantine, a combination of bronze and ivory (see p.102). However, Preiss also made a few all-ivory figures, often small Classical female nudes. The quality of his carving was usually very high. Many of his figures are teutonic, Aryan types with tinted naturalistic faces and stained hair. He specialized in sporting figures, some based on real sportsmen and sportswomen, and actresses. Most Preiss figures are less than 14 in high (35.5cm). They usually bear the "PK" monogram (for the Preiss-Kassler foundry), and the signature "F. Preiss".
* Preiss mass-produced an Aryan-type figure in which all the parts were carved separately and screwed to the bronze, and were individually finished.

Value Points
* Preiss figures on ashtrays or dish-mounted tend to be less desirable than figures on bases.
* Preiss' ivory child sculptures are not as desirable as the chryselephantine or female studies, and are generally regarded as small cabinet-fillers.

Beware
As with the work of other top sculptors of the period, copies exist. These often use a softer type of stone which resembles onyx. Be suspicious of any figures attributed to Preiss that have a very elaborate base.

The Preiss-Kassler Foundry
The company was formed in Berlin in 1906. Preiss himself designed most of the models produced by the firm although by 1914 there were about six designers working for him. The factory closed during the First World War, but reopened in 1919, and by the middle of the next decade employed about ten designers. In 1929 Preiss-Kassler took over the firm and the sculptors of Rosenthal und Maeder (RuM).
Preiss-Kassler sculptors included:
* Rudolf Belling
* Dorothea Charol
* Walter Kassler
* R. W. Lange
* Philip Lenz
* Paul Philippe
* Otto Poertzel (see *right*)
* Ludwig Walter

RECREATIONAL THEMES
Figures of the Art Deco period generally tend to convey a sense of living life to the full. Many are engaged in what would have been considered "modern" activities, often reflecting women's release from demure stillness and decorative inactivity. A range of sports and pastimes were depicted, especially:
* dancing
* snake charming and acrobatics
* swimming/bathing
* smoking
* golf, skiing and tennis
* skating
* javelin throwing
* fishing

OTTO POERTZEL

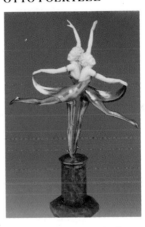

For many years controversy has surrounded some figures which emanated from the P.K. factory and are marked "Prof Poertzel", such as the figure *above*, known as *The Twins* or *Butterfly Dancers*. These bear such a resemblance to the work of Preiss that it was suggested Preiss used the name Poertzel as a pseudonym. However, it is now believed that Poertzel worked at Preiss's foundry. Poertzel figures are usually chryselephantine and, unlike some by Preiss, seldom appear in all-ivory. Some figures emanating from the Preiss-Kassler foundry bear Preiss's and Poertzel's signature. Although the figure here is signed by Poertzel, an almost identical example bears Preiss' signature, and another version has both names.

DEMETRE CHIPARUS

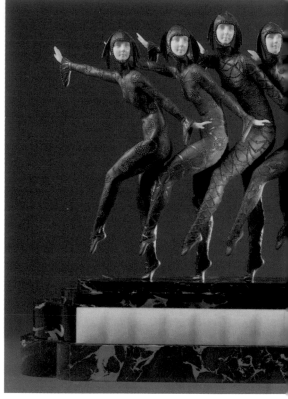

The Girls, *a gilt and cold-painted bronze and ivory group by Demetre Chiparus c.1930; ht 20in/52cm, lgth 24in/62cm with base; value code A*

Identification checklist for the sculpture of Chiparus
1. Are the costumes elaborate and tight-fitting – for example, cat suits or skull caps?
2. Does the sculpture have an exotic or science-fiction look?
3. Is the pose theatrical?
4. Does the base have a sculptural quality, and perhaps an architectural marble or onyx plinth?
5. Is there an Etling foundry mark?
6. Is the material chryselephantine (an expensive and highly desirable combination of bronze and ivory)?

Condition
This is crucial to any assessment of value; the extremities of many figures have suffered from knocks and chips. Ivory is especially susceptible to being damaged and is also prone to cracking: this is particularly detrimental to value where the cracks extend down the face, giving the piece a disfiguring black-veined appearance.

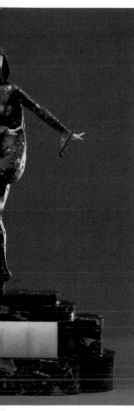

Demetre Chiparus
(Romanian, dates unknown)

Although born in Romania, Chiparus worked in Paris. Many of his early figures were produced by the Parisian company, Etling (see p. 55). Some later works were produced by the LN & JL foundry. Chiparus was the chief exponent of chryselephantine, a highly desirable combination of bronze and ivory. He specialized in depicting exotic women, many inspired by the *Ballets Russes,* popular in Paris between c.1917 and c.1920. Inspiration was also provided by other contemporary figures and shows. Many of his sculptures exhibit Mexican, Inca, Aztec or Mayan influences. Nudes are uncommon. Some pieces were made in more than one size or in both bronze and chryselephantine.

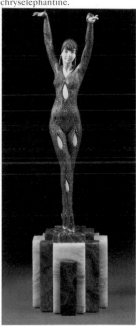

Beware

Fakes of chryselephantine figures have appeared on the market, including some made of plastic. Examine the following:
* The quality of casting and carving, and the subtlety of joints.
* The graining of any ivory (although recently fakes made from artificially grained plastic or "ivorene" have appeared).
* The facial tint; this should be subtle, possibly showing signs of age. Be suspicious of garish, modern-looking paint, but don't rule it out altogether – the sculpture may have been retouched.
* The gilt surface, which should have acquired a patination, hard to reproduce artificially.
* The original figures were sometimes secured to the base by wing nuts; the fakes invariably use an ordinary screw and nut.

Elaborate bases, such as this one, are typical of Chiparus. Many of his sculptu[...] plaques wh[...] theme of t[...] nearly alwa[...] the base. T[...] "DH. chipa[...] "ETLING,[...] *above,* bears[...] Chiparaus".[...]

s[...]
An[...]
simp,[...]
differen[...]
(61cm), w.[...]
and no brass[...]
the inscription.[...]
108

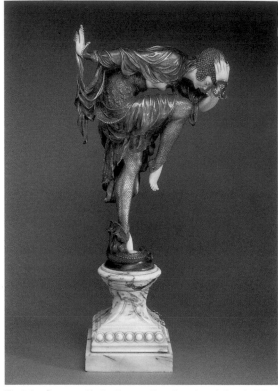

The Ankara Dancer, *a cold-painted bronze and ivory figure of a snake dancer by Colinet c.1925; ht 13in/25.5cm; value code B*

Identification checklist for the sculpture of Colinet
1. Is the costume flowing and elaborate?
2. Does the figure embody a strong sense of movement?
3. Does the sculpture have an Eastern flavour?
4. Is the subject idealized?
5. Are women generously proportioned (in contrast to the more streamlined figures of Chiparus, see pp. 106-7)?
6. Do women convey a sense of the femme fatale?

Claire-Jeanne-Roberte Colinet, Belgian (dates, unknown)
Colinet is mainly known for her series of dancers. Several versions were made of the same figure. ...gnatures vary – for example, the *...ra Dancer above* is inscribed ... "Cl.J.R. Colinet 13". A ... edition, 24 inches high ... h a green marble base ... ggings, and bearing ... "C.J.R. Colinet", is stamped "42 Made in France", and impressed with the LN & JL foundry seal, with a separate brass tag inscribed "DANSEUSE D'ANKARA Par Cl.J.R. COLINET".

In addition to dancers, Colinet depicted a number of mythical and historic figures, such as Narcissus, Cupid, Joan of Arc, and a crusader. These are less collectable and therefore less expensive.

Dancers of the world

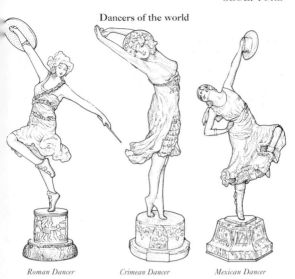

Roman Dancer   *Crimean Dancer*   *Mexican Dancer*

Each dancer has a title plaque. The bas relief on the base often reflects the nationality of the dancer, usually a dramatic idealized figure. Dancers often hold an emblem typical of the country they represent, such as the sombrero brandished by the Mexican dancer. Other figures in the series include the Hindu dancer and the Egyptian dancer.

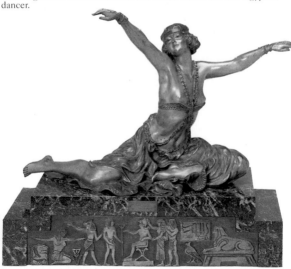

Most of the dancers are of chryselephantine, with a gilt or cold-painted surface, or a combination of the two. Bases are either onyx or marble or, very occasionally, alabaster. This *Theban Dancer* on a marble base is unusual in being of patinated bronze, although there is a more expensive version in chryselephantine. Fakes are known to exist.
* It is not known precisely how many dancers were in the series, as new ones are still being identified.

MARCEL BOURAINE

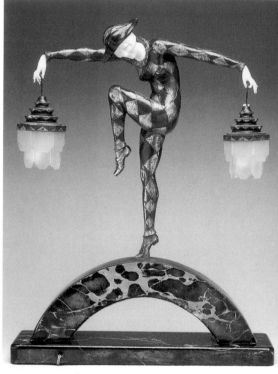

Harlequin, *a Bouraine bronze, ivory and glass table lamp c.1925; ht 25in/60cm; value code B*

Identification checklist for Bouraine sculpture
1. Is the subject a figure from history or mythology, or a dancer or clown?
2. Does the piece bear a signature on the base or plinth, and the inscription of the Etling foundry in Paris?
3. Is there a geometrically elaborate base, perhaps of streaked or patinated black marble? (Onyx, brass and bronze were also common.)
4. Is the pose exaggerated and dramatic, perhaps with the subject depicted balanced on one leg?
5. Is the figure of bronze or chryselephantine?
6. Is there a multimedia effect, with elaborate appliqué details?
7. Is there a sense of muscular strength or windswept movement?

Note
Some figures were made in more than one size and with minor variations to decorative details.

Marcel Bouraine (French, dates unknown)

Bouraine is best known for his chryselephantine figures, made during the inter-War years, and for his groups cast fully in bronze. Amazons were popular (see *below*), also sporting and mythical figures. Some wear two-dimensional formalized draperies. Many others are nude. Groups often contain animal as well as human figures, especially hunting dogs, swans or other birds.

Bouraine's sculptures are distinctive for their use of a variety of media combined in one piece. Patinas of gold and bronze were often employed, some including enamelled, silvered or stencilled surfaces, and garlanded with carved, sometimes painted ivory.

Marks and authenticity

Bouraine sculptures are usually marked. Much of his work was commissioned and distributed by the Parisian firm Etling (see p. 55), whose marks often accompany the sculptor's signature. The harlequin shown *opposite* is stamped "BRONZE FRANCE", signed "BOURAINE", and inscribed "ETLING, PARIS". The underside is inscribed "MADE IN FRANCE".

No fakes are known to exist. The French glass artist and ceramist Gabriel Argy-Rousseau (see pp. 48-9) created statuettes in pâte de verre during the 1930s after Bouraine's designs. These have the incised signature of G. Argy-Rousseau on the base.

Many Bouraine figures are portrayed with outstretched arms and holding some kind of prop, such as a hoop, bow, spear or, as with this bronze dancer of the 1920s, a fan.
* The complicated, partially stepped, yellow-veined marble plinth supporting the fan dancer is typical, as is the use of several media and colours: the fan is cold-painted in silver, gold, blue and white.

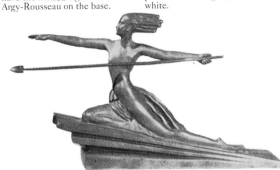

A recurring subject in Bouraine's work was the streamlined, naked Amazonian figure or Diana-like huntress, with windswept hair, frozen in the motion of running, hunting or throwing a spear, as in the bronze archer *above*.
* Bouraine's Amazonian women are invariably powerful, detailed and realistic.

111

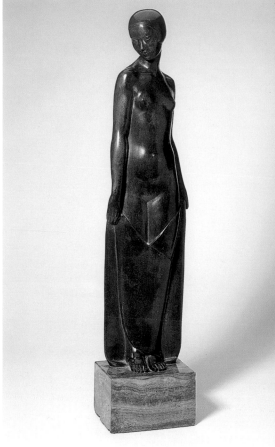

A bronze female figure by Pierre Le Faguays
c.1925; 24in/61cm; value code C

Identification checklist for the sculpture of Pierre le Faguays

1. Is the figure delicately poised, or simplified and serene?
2. Is the piece marked "Le Faguays"?
3. Is the material bronze, possibly silvered or combined with ivory?
4. Is the human form precisely and accurately sculpted?
5. Does the bronze have a damascened pattern similar to that used by Bouraine? (See pp. 110-11.)
6. Is the subject a single figure?
7. Is the base in black striated marble, or black and green onyx?

...e Faguays worked in three distinct idioms. The most successful and desirable of these is his female studies, which have a strong element of stylization: in the example shown, *left*, hair is represented as a skullcap, the features are prominent and simplified, and the pose is serene. Typically of this group of sculptures, there is a distinct feeling of stillness and serenity, with arms and legs held close to the body – a style that is very different from that of other craftsmen working in this period.

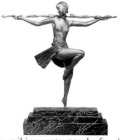

In striking contrast to the female study on the opposite page, this 1930s Le Faguays *Dancer with Thyrsus* is shown in a typical Art Deco period pose. The sculpture is one of a group of works by this artist that depict the more conventionally Art Deco woman – often nude or scantily clad, and shown dancing or as a harem girl or warrior. Many are given formal draperies, or something to hold: garlands of flowers or musical instruments.

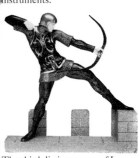

The third distinct group of Le Faguays figures is that depicting idealized mythological or allegorical figures, such as this 1930s archer, *Signal Man, above*, which shows Le Faguays high-quality draughtsmanship and attention to anatomical accuracy.

Pierre Le Faguays (French, b.1892)

A leading sculptor of the Art Deco period, Le Faguays produced work for Arthur Goldscheider's Parisian foundry (which outlasted its Austrian parent company) in the 1920s, and exhibited under Goldscheider's "La Stele" label at the Paris Exhibition in 1925. He also worked for the house of Le Verrier, making decorative items for sale through Max Le Verrier's shop in Paris.

Materials

Many of Le Faguays' sculptures and most of the larger ones are in bronze; smaller pieces may include ivory. He also worked in wood, stone and silvered bronze. All-ivory figures are rare. Some of his sculptures incorporate cold-painted colors – for example, the *Dancer with Floral Skirt*. Others occasionally incorporate slightly unusual materials, such as alabaster and rouge marble, used in *The Puppet Theatre*.
* The bases of Le Faguays sculptures are in a variety of materials; especially popular were black striated marble and black and green onyx.

Marks

The sculptures are usually signed "Le Faguays". This may be carved or incise-cast into the base. Some bear the foundry mark "LNJL Paris", and may carry a design number.
* Pieces displayed at the 1925 Paris Exhibition carry the "La Stele" foundry seal as well as Le Faguays' name.

Collecting

Although Le Faguays was relatively prolific, his work does not come up for sale as frequently as pieces by Preiss, Chiparus, Colinet or Lorenzl. His sculptures are more readily available in France than elsewhere. Some of his pieces incorporate jardinières or are fitted with electricity for lighting and these command a premium (as do any items from the period with a utilitarian as well as a decorative value). The largest group – the dancers and harem figures, which represents Le Faguays' more commercial side, are perhaps slightly less sought-after than the serene and more individual sculptures like that shown on the opposite page; these, were not made in large numbers.

113

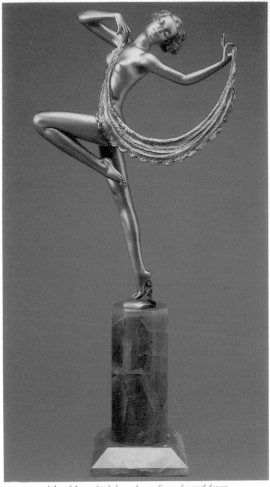

A Joseph Lorenzl polychrome bronze figure of a scarf dancer. c.1928; ht 28¹/₂in/72.5cm including base; value code C

Identification checklist for the sculpture of Lorenzl
1. Is the figure stylized, with a dramatic posture?
2. Are the limbs unnaturally elongated to suggest elegance, rather than being strictly accurate?
3. Is the subject female and either naked or in a skin-tight mini-dress?
4. Is she poised on one leg, possibly with an outstretched arm?
5. Does the sculpture stand on a pedestal?
6. Is the base onyx?
7. Is the piece signed?

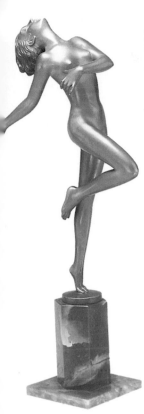

Joseph Lorenzl (Austrian, dates unknown)

One of the leading sculptors of the Art Deco period, Lorenzl produced a range of figures in bronze, ivory, and occasionally in chryselephantine (an expensive and highly desirable combination of bronze and ivory).

Lorenzl's sculptures usually depict single white females, and tend to be fairly small – up to 12 inches (30.5cm) without the pedestal. Unusually for sculptors of the period, Lorenzl seldom depicted figures from antiquity or the theatre. However, his females have the 20s or 30s look, with bobbed or cropped hair. They tend to be very slim with streamlined figures and small breasts and are usually idealized, although the facial features are realistic, with serene, calm expressions. The nudes often hold a scarf, fan or other accessory. Many of the subjects are dancers, usually naked and in acrobatic positions.

Lorenzl favoured a patinated silver or gilt finish with additional enamel colouring on the scarves, hair and so on, and it is this which gives the figures their characteristic metallic look.

As with the work of some other sculptors of the period, figures were often produced in a range of sizes.

The bases of Lorenzl's sculptures are usually faceted and of plain onyx, although black slate and marble were occasionally used.

Lorenzl's work is not believed to have been faked.

* Plaster and ceramic versions of Lorenzl bronzes (and those of other important sculptors of the day, such as Bruno Zach,) were produced by the Austrian-based firm Friedrich Goldscheider (see p. 95).

Note
It has often been assumed that the dull surface of patinated figures, such as those by Lorenzl, is caused by dirt. Consequently, many of them have been polished to such an extent that their patinated top surface has been rubbed away. This is very detrimental to value.

* "Cast from a model by", is a term sometimes used in auction house catalogues to indicate that the figure is not the original model.

The green onyx base of this typical Lorenzl bronze figure of a naked woman bears the signature "Lorenzl". Lorenzl used a variety of signatures, which were usually permutations of his name. The most commonly found examples include:
* "Lorenzl" in full, which is the most common of his signatures.
* "Lor", on small pieces, when it is usually found under the skirt or under the foot.
* "Renzl".
Script lettering is commonly used on taller pieces, generally on the domed base. Capital letters, usually on smaller pieces, are found on the perimeter of the flat base.
* The painted mark "Crejo" appears on some partially painted figures.
* Some of Lorenzl's sculptures are numbered, but the numbers are not considered significant by collectors.

BRUNO ZACH

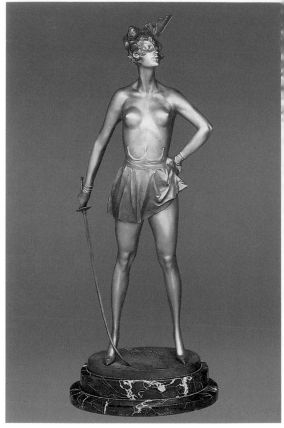

A Bruno Zach polychrome figure of a fencer
c.1930; ht 28¹/₂in/72.5cm; value code C

Identification checklist for Zach sculpture
1. Is the subject risqué?
2. If a woman, is the figure semi-naked, with an amazonian or provocative pose and a haughty expression?
3. Do any women have hair that is bobbed, or tied with a bow?
4. Is there a sense of movement to any clothes, which may also be in a contrasting patination?
5. Does the subject have an idealized figure?
6. Is the base of fairly plain black or grey marble with fine cream striations?
7. Is there an incised signature cast into the top of the base?

Bruno Zach, (Austrian, dates unknown)

Little is known of the life of this sculptor, famous for his erotic, slightly prurient portraits of the Berlin *demi-monde*. Among his lesser known works are some sporting figures, such as skiers, which are not as collectable as the erotic subjects.

Zach's subjects are nearly always female. Multiple figures are rare, but pairs exist, usually of dancers or lovers. Women often hold riding crops or whips. Most stand with their legs slightly apart in an affirmative stance, rather than in the ladylike pose typical of many figures of the period. These are not the jewel-adorned playthings often depicted in the 1920s and 30s, but have a certain severity uncharacteristic of sculptures at the time. It is not uncommon for Zach's dancing figures to be poised on one leg.

Zach accurately depicted the costume of the period. This is helpful for dating, as some items, such as pyjama suits and camisoles, were not introduced until 1920. The costumes also contribute to the sensual impression given by the figures – for example, garters, and full length gloves (although these are not useful for dating, as they were worn from the end of the 19thC). Some figures wear leather clothing. Most have shoes or boots – even if they are otherwise naked or scantily clad.

Zach worked mostly in bronze or chryselephantine. He favoured gilt patination, and very occasionally used patinated bronze. Ivory was often contrasted with black patination. He also made a few cold-painted pieces.

Well-known Zach figures include:
* *The Riding Crop* (in bronze and bronze and ivory)
* *The Cigarette Girl*

Cold-painted or metallic patination?

Cold-painting, popularized by Franz Bergman, was largely an Austrian practice. Whereas most Art Deco figures of the period were finished with a metallic patination, obtained by exposing the metal to the fumes of various chemicals, Bergman used coloured enamels, which were annealed or painted on to the figure.

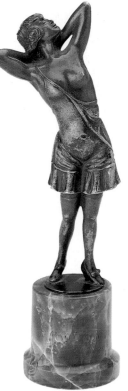

Zach's work is nearly always signed with his big bold signature. Some unsigned pieces have been attributed to him, but unless the piece is marked it should not be accepted as Zach without the evidence of contemporary documentation. Copies abound: these are distinguished by their poor-quality casting and patination, apparent in the pseudo-Zach figure, *above*, which satisfies few of the requirements suggested by the checklist. This somewhat unappealing copy has an ungraceful, almost dumpy figure, and is neither sensual nor erotic. The proportions of the body are wrong – there is even the suggestion of a paunch! The posture is a little awkward and unflattering and the costume is rather static. The base is thinner than in genuine Zach figures, and the pedestal, although striated, is green onyx, which was rarely used by Zach.

117

PAUL MANSHIP

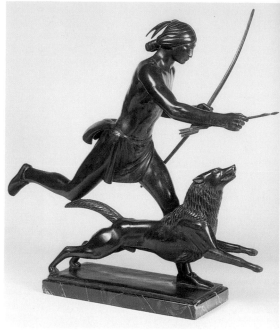

A bronze sculpture by Paul Manship entitled Indian hunter and his dog
1926; ht 21³/₄in/55.25 cm; value code B

Identification checklist for the sculpture of Paul Manship
1. Is the form fluid and lively?
2. Is the figural modelling precise, with sharp features?
3. Are the quality of casting and patination of the bronze of the highest standard?
4. Is there an impressed foundry mark?
5. Is the base comparatively simple in form?
6. Is the work suitable for production on a large, architectural scale?

Paul Howard Manship
(American, 1885-1966)
Manship studied art at some of the major colleges of the early 20thC, including New York (where he worked with the animalier Solon Borglun), Pennsylvania, and Rome. He was very impressed by the work of the French sculptor Auguste Rodin and his followers, and by classical sculpture, which was to prove influential in his later work. By 1912 Manship had developed a style and standard of modelling which combined the new thought

of the Rodin school with Classical principles of realism and scale, and which became associated with an entire movement of American sculpture of the 1920s and 30s. Manship's first exhibition in New York brought him instant acclaim, and he went on to enjoy a level of commercial success extraordinary for a 20thC sculptor.

Marks
All Manship's pieces are inscribed with his signature, usually including a copyright mark and the date.

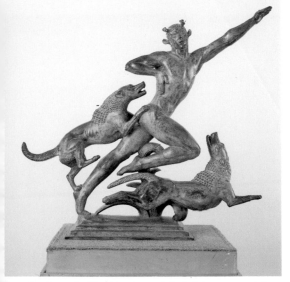

Several sculptures by Manship take mythological characters as their subject: this bronze group from 1925 entitled *Acteon*, was designed to accompany another similarly dramatic bronze group *Diana*.

* The most famous of Manship's mythological sculptures is that of Prometheus, installed as a centrepiece in the Rockefeller Centre in New York in 1934.

* Some of Manship's medals also have mythological subjects – for example *Hail to Dionysus* (1930).

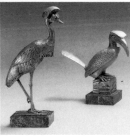

Manship's bronze sculpture in the Art Deco style was not limited to statuary. He produced a number of medals and medallions and, during the 1920s, cast a menagerie of animal sculpture, much of it stylized in the subtly geometric, Cubist-inspired fashion favoured by French sculptors such as Édouard Sandoz (see p. 123). The range includes a collection of ten exotic birds, among them this crowned crane and concave-casqued hornbill. The range, commissioned by the Bronx Zoo, also included other animals.

Style

Manship's work is characterized by its repeat-pattern techniques and use of flat, controlled drapery. There is an emphasis on linear elegance, expressed in stylized hair and draperies and clarity of contour. Later, 1930s works show a more streamlined, but equally vigorous Modernism.

Most Manship sculpture was cast by American foundries, notably the Roman Bronze Works in New York. The piece in the main picture is unusual as it bears the foundry stamp of Alexis Ruder, Paris.

Smaller works

Much of Manship's small sculpture was produced commercially in limited editions as reductions of large-scale works, many of which had been public commissions. The figure *Indian Hunter and His Dog* in the main picture was originally cast as a life-size fountain of the same title, which was commissioned in 1925.

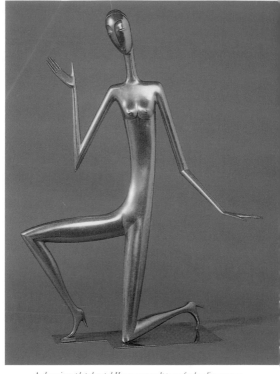

A chromium-plated metal Hagenauer sculpture of a kneeling woman c.1928; ht 35½in/90.5cm; value code D

Identification checklist for Hagenauer sculpture
1. Are any figures stylized and streamlined?
2. Are animal and human faces almost mask-like?
3. Is the sculpture made of silver, chromium-plated bronze, or brass?
4. Is the monogram "wHw" of the Hagenauer Vienna Workshop stamped onto the base, or, if there is no base, on the underside of the body in an unobtrusive position?
5. Do any figures or animals combine flowing curves with clean angles and elongated tapering limbs?
6. Is the sculpture either self-supporting or mounted on a minimal thin metal silver-coloured base?
7. Is the surface smooth without decoration, carving or other embellishment?
8. Do animal and human forms display a sense of movement?
9. Even if the main subject is not figural, do figures appear somewhere, perhaps at the base of a lamp or bowl?

Hagenauer (Austrian, established 1898)

The Hagenauer Werkstätte (Workshop) was founded in Vienna in 1898 by Carl Hagenauer (1872-1928). Initially it specialized in practical and ornamental artefacts – metal tablewares, lamps, mirrors and vases – but it became famous for the metal figurines and groups of the 1910-30 period, which were exhibited throughout Europe.

Carl Hagenauer's eldest son Karl joined the firm in 1919 and, together with his brother Franz, took over in 1928. In the 1930s their designs were at the forefront of the New Realism.

Form and decoration
The movement of the piece, whether a dancer, gymnast, horse or panther, is conveyed by simple unbroken design, pared of superfluous detail. Form often merges into function: horse-riders into lamp-stands, arms and hands into brackets for candelabra and book-ends. The decoration is also contained within the form, rather than being applied to it. Sculptures are usually of bronze, copper or brass, or of a wood (often ebony) and metal combination, or chrome.

Collecting Hagenauer
It is difficult to distinguish between the work of the three principal Hagenauers. However, Carl and Karl were largely responsible for the utilitarian wares, while Franz specialized in decorative sculptures, such as the two-dimensionally stylized *The Boxers*, illustrated *right*.
* Hagenauer masks are particularly sought after, as well as those figures with a Modigliani or Brancusi influence. Usually, the more decorative and stylish the piece, the more collectable it is.

Marks
The pieces are usually stamped with the Hagenauer monogram "wHw" and sometimes the designer's name, the date, and place of origin.

Note
Wood and bronze was a favourite combination in figures from c.1910 until the mid-20s. Pieces from this period were of an avant-garde, highly stylized design, becoming more realistic and detailed in the 1930s.

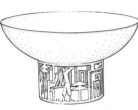

A brass-footed bowl with a figured base, designed by Karl Hagenauer

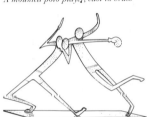

A mounted polo player, cast in brass

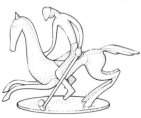

The boxers, *a highly stylized brass sculpture designed by Franz Hagenauer*

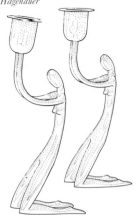

A pair of Hagenauer brass candlesticks cast as stylized kneeling female figures, stamped "wHw, made in Austria."

121

FRANÇOIS POMPON

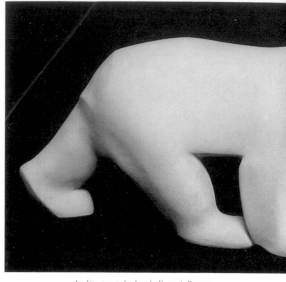

A white stone polar bear by François Pompon
c.1930; ht 10in/25.5cm, lgth 18in/45.7cm; value code A/B

Identification checklist for the sculpture of François Pompon
1. Is the piece signed?
2. Is it stylized?
3. Is the surface smooth?
4. Does the patination complement the subject?
5. Is the subject an animal?
6. Is the figure freestanding?
7. Does the form convey a sense of movement?

François Pompon (French, 1855-1933)
Pompon was one of the leading animaliers of the period. Inspired by the impressionistic work of Rembrandt Bugatti, and the bird and animal etchings of Paul Jouve, both of whom worked in the early years of the 20thC, Pompon created a number of important animal sculptures, including the polar bear shown *above* – his most famous sculpture – exhibited at the Paris Exhibition when Pompon was 67. Pompon's work was highly stylized. He paid particular attention to the finish, making good use of patination. He particularly favoured a mirror-black finish when working in bronze. The polar bear uses the colour of the stone to maximum effect. Surfaces were often highly polished. Although his figures are so stylized, Pompon nevertheless manages to suggest a sense of movement: compare the walking bear with the static seated monkey by Sandoz, shown *right*. Pompon worked on a few model portraits and on outdoor sculpture, but collectors today are primarily interested in his animals. His work is usually signed underneath with the word "POMPON". Few fakes are known.
* It is not unusual for Pompon's animals to be freestanding, although most animal sculptures of the period stand on marble bases.

122

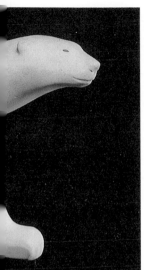

Art Deco animals

Certain animals feature strongly in Art Deco sculpture. They include:

* The panther, the most popular Deco animal. Panthers are shown singly and in packs.
* The gazelle, second to the panther in popularity. This is often depicted with Diana the huntress, or with seabirds, especially albatrosses and gulls. French sculptures sometimes show gulls on the tip of a wave.
* Dogs; these exemplify the spirit of the age, particularly borzois, which were popular because they are sleek and fast. Perhaps the best known is Poertzel's *Aristocrats* featuring a medieval lady with two borzois.
* Birds, including Oriental pheasants and fan-tail doves.
* Fish (especially Lalique).
* Cats, now very collectable. Bookends often took the form of pairs of animals, such as pelicans, unicorns and seals. Cats also appeared as car mascots.

Other animal sculptors

A. Becquerel (including mascots)
Marcel Bouraine
Alex Kéléty
G. H. Laurent (including bookends)
Max Le Verrier
Paul Manship (especially birds)

EDOUARD MARCEL SANDOZ,
(Swiss, 1881-1971)

After Pompon, Sandoz is probably the most important animalier of the period (his monuments and portraits are generally regarded as works of lesser importance). He broke away both from the highly naturalistic presentation of many of the French animaliers, and from the impressionistic work of Bugatti and Pompon: instead he favoured a more formalized approach.

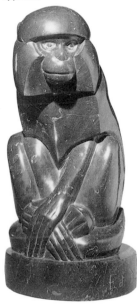

This black marble seated monkey is typical of Sandoz in its still, brooding attitude, and in having an almost human expression. The somewhat static posture is even more pronounced in his bookends. Some of Sandoz's work is unusually small, less than 1½in (3.8 cm) tall, and appears in glazed porcelain and biscuit, as well as marble. His animals are usually mounted on marble bases. Many have expressions, sometimes humorous. Sandoz was close to Bouraine (see pp. 110-11) in his treatment of animal subjects.

* Animal sculptures were also produced in the United States, by such designers as Cornelia Chapin. Many were intended for gardens. (see pp. 118-19.)

MINOR SCULPTURE

The works shown on the preceding pages represent the best sculptures that the period has to offer, and as such they tend to be very expensive. However, there is a fair amount of less expensive sculpture from the 1920s and 30s on the market. Some of these wares have simply yet to become appreciated; others may rise in value as more details emerge about the craftsmen. There are also pieces that lack either the technical perfection or the quality of materials that typify the best pieces.

Some relatively inexpensive works are still available in bronze and sometimes even in chryselephantine (see p. 102) and these usually represent better value than those sculptures made in spelter, a zinc alloy introduced in the early 20thC. However, by the 1920s and 30s some quite attractive spelter figures were also being made.

The forms of many lesser sculptures are usually simple and employ the minimum of casting – for example, the fingers may not be separated, and feet are often cast as one block. Facial features may also be poorly executed, with bland expressions.
* Spelter is easily scratched and the white metal often shows through. It also fractures more easily than bronze. Natural wear may cause it to oxidize and form a series of bubbles on the surface, popularly known as "spelter disease". Once these bubbles or fractures occur, they are very difficult to repair.

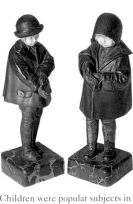

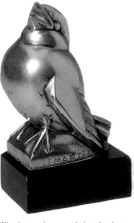

Children were popular subjects in 1900-25. These two French bronze-gilded chryselephantine figures, c.1925, are evocative of the period, with stained ivory bobbed hair and typical 1920s costume.

The quality of the casting is good, as is that of the ivory. The bases are good-quality chamfered and polished striated marble.

These figures are relatively inexpensive examples of their type because of their size (they are only about 8in (20cm) high), and the obscurity of their artist (who has signed the figures with the name "Fath"). Their desirability is also reduced by their limited decorative appeal and their lack of drama.

The heavy base and simple shape of this silvered bronze bird, signed Martel, suggest that it may have been designed as a bookend. Figures of small birds were popular during this period: the form of this one follows Sandoz and Lalique in its simplicity. However, this example is not particularly endearing: it is somewhat static and lacks charm. The standard of craftsmanship is not high: the silvering is distressed and worn, and the plate is wearing through. The black Belgian slate base is plain and cheap.

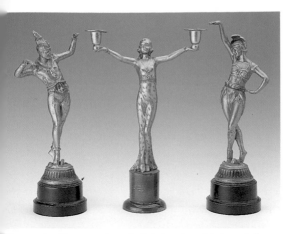

These spelter figures are thematically in keeping with the period. Some attempt has been made to introduce a futuristic element into the two outer figures, but the costumes are contrived, and all three pieces lack finesse. They are somewhat inelegant and convey little sense of movement. The postures seem unlikely and even absurd. The finish is gaudy and relatively unattractive, even though some attempt has been made to simulate gilt bronze with staining. The bases of the two dancers are bakelite, in imitation of marble, while the girl in the centre stands on a stained wood base – the cheapest type of all. The figures have not worn well: the sconce of one of the candlesticks has bent, and the stained finish is wearing away.

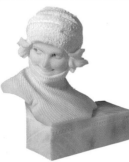

This carved Italian piece is in alabaster, a relatively inexpensive soft stone which scratches easily. Prices are therefore quite low, even for attractive, well-carved sculptures such as this representation of a contemporary skier. The off-centre position of the girl gives the work a slightly awkward appearance, but the carving is good (the sweater is technically very clever), and the overall proportions are excellent. The facial features are well-defined and the girl's expression appealing – an important factor for many collectors.

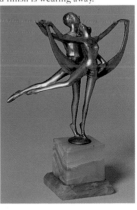

These dancers recall the work of Lorenzl (see pp. 114-15), but they are less accomplished in the following ways:
* the posture is contrived and the faces bland
* there is minimal definition
* the gilt bronze shows poor casting – for example, the skirt joins the girl's hand
* patination is poorly controlled
* the base, although onyx, is very simple in form.

125

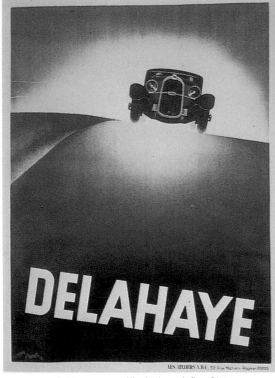

Delahaye, *an automobile advertisement by Roger Pérot*

In the 1920s and 30s posters were used primarily as an advertising medium to promote travel, art exhibitions and sports meetings, as well as occasionally for political propaganda. Poster designs of the period are unfussy, and the emphasis is on a strong central image. Colours were brighter than before, and new typefaces were employed.

The most striking images of the period are by French artists, the most innovative of whom was Cassandre (see p. 128-9), who used strong colours and an unusual sense of perspective. Paul Colin is the most important name in the area of theatre advertising, and is known for his posters advertising the actress Josephine Baker. Other major artists who worked on posters include Erté (see p. 134-5) and Jean Dupas (see p. 130-31), many of whose lithographs have been converted into posters. Works by Icart were intended to be purely decorative: he produced no posters for advertising.

In Britain London Transport commissioned a series of posters from a number of leading artists. Subjects are often shown following the pursuits of the day, especially playing golf, and visiting places made more accessible by the railways – for example, seaside resorts. In the United States Maxfield Parrish created posters reminiscent of the Art Nouveau style, but making use of more brilliant and unusual colours.

Film posters, now keenly contested by poster collectors and film enthusiasts, are an area that grew with the development of Hollywood. They are in colour, often using two-tone artwork, and many are by unknown artists. Few have survived, although they were originally produced in large numbers (every cinema would have had one).

Magazine covers and prints taken from magazines, described in some auction catalogues as "printed ephemera" are currently very inexpensive. The original artwork is occasionally available, but is rare and usually commands a high price. Many European designers worked for American magazines such as *Harper's Bazaar* and *Vogue*.

Images were reproduced in a number of ways: collectors are likely to find references in auction house catalogues to posters, prints, lithographs and drypoint and etching, and sometimes to the original artworks. Engravings and etchings are produced on copperplate. Engraving is done with a knife straight onto the plate; in etching the plate is covered with wax, the design drawn into it, then the whole plate dipped in acid, which eats into the areas not covered by the wax. The result looks more like a drawing; engravings have a more stilted appearance, and an embossed effect. Lithographs are made by applying wax or an ink-resistant chemical to a stone surface, which is then covered with ink, so that exposed areas are coloured while others are left untouched. The ink lies on the surface which, unlike an etching, is completely flat. Photogravure is used to reproduce an etching or engraving: the item is photographed and the photographic negative applied to copper plate; the image is then etched or engraved. When photogravures are examined under a magnifier, the image is revealed as a matrix of tiny dots.

Prints and posters are not prone to being faked. Modern reproductions, which abound, are easy to detect as they are invariably executed on thicker paper with a glossy coated surface, and exhibit none of the characteristic signs of age of a 60- or 70-year old work.

Condition is crucial to value. Pieces with tears and creases – especially those that interfere with the central image rather than the border – command a substantially reduced price, and unless the work is exceptionally rare are probably not worth buying at all. However, few posters from the period have survived completely undamaged as, not being intended as collectors' items, they were printed on poor-quality paper. The kinds of damage that are acceptable include minor fading or some loss of the paper around the edges. Some auction houses use letters to denote condition, ranging from "A" for those in very good condition, through to "D" for serious damage. Collectors prefer unmounted pictures: avoid those that have been applied to board.

ADOLPHE J. M. CASSANDRE

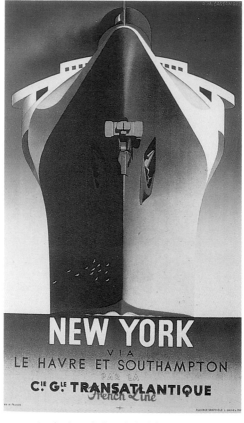

An advertisement by Cassandre for the liner Normandie
1936; 24 x 39in/613 x 99cm; value code B/C

Identification checklist for the posters of Cassandre
1. Is perspective used to dramatic effect?
2. Does the poster use shading to create an impression of movement?
3. Is the poster signed?
4. Is it avant-garde, making use of strong images and bold lettering?
5. Does it show machinery of any kind?

Adolphe J. M. Cassandre (French, 1901-68)
Cassandre was born Jean-Marie Mouron, but adopted the pseudonym at the beginning of his career. He was one of the first to take up the language of formal art movements such as Cubism and apply them to the more popular medium of the advertising poster. He is best known for his striking travel posters, many of which show ships and trains.

128

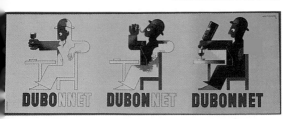

Cassandre's work is often humorous and innovative, as in his *Dubonnet* poster from 1934. The product itself is not shown, but its effect is depicted using a cartoon-strip technique.

Style and technique

Cassandre's distinctive graphic style uses bright colours combined with subtle shading to give subjects a metallic impression and a sense of speed – a popular preoccupation during this period. His use of perspective is also distinctive and possibly shows a Japanese influence through simplification and elimination of superfluous details. Images are often stark and forceful: the poster shown *left*, celebrates the modernity of the ship, rather than emphasizing the luxurious aspects of the cruise.

Lettering is often bold, clear type, usually sans serif – without cross lines finishing off the strokes of the letters.

Collecting

Although Cassandre's work includes posters, lithographs and cover designs for the magazine *Harper's Bazaar*, his original designs and drawings are not usually available. Even the posters are quite scarce. (In recent years they have most frequently been found in poster sales in New York.) Of his three best-known works, that advertising the liner *Normandie* commands a top price, followed by that for the *Etoile du Nord* railway service, which uses an abstract interpretation of railway tracks to give a feeling of speed, space and distance. The poster for the *Nord Express* railway service also commands a good price.

Quality

The technical execution of the print tends to be masterful: surface brush or collage marks are usually invisible, and it is even difficult to distinguish hand lettering from type.

PAUL COLIN (French, 1892-1985)

Like Cassandre, this French artist designed travel posters, but his work also includes theatre programme covers and posters advertising performers as well as cigarettes and other products. In 1926 he opened the École Paul Colin. He is best known for his posters to advertise visiting jazz musicians at the *Folies Bergères* and other venues, and for his 1925 series on the actress Josephine Baker, who was appearing in the *Revue Nègre*. His often light-hearted illustrative style is neither as austere nor as sophisticated as that of Cassandre, nor is his work as collectable.

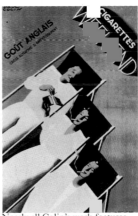

Nearly all Colin's work features human figures, sometimes highly stylized, sometimes caricatured. This cigarette poster from c.1936 showing three smart smokers in deck chairs, is typical of Colin's spirited, angular style and shows how his work epitomizes important aspects of the 1920s/30s poster generally in its:
* overhead view
* composition tilted towards the diagonal
* use of strong colours in unlikely combinations.

129

JEAN DUPAS

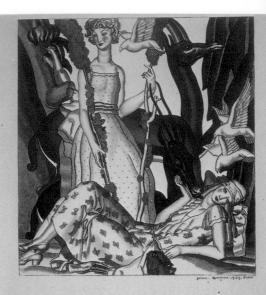

A Jean Dupas fashion poster
1929; 35$^{1}/_2$ x 47$^{1}/_2$in/90 x 120cm; value code C

Identification checklist for the work of Dupas
1. Are figures highly stylized, with elongated features?
2. Is the setting idyllic, possibly showing a Classical influence?
3. Are the colours relatively subdued?
4. Is the work signed and dated?
5. Does the picture include animals?
6. Is any lettering separate from the image?

Jean Dupas (French, 1882-1964)
Dupas was a painter and poster artist who trained at the major Paris schools. His work includes posters, catalogue covers and large murals.

Dupas designed posters for a variety of clients. His work includes a series of advertisements for the American department store Saks Fifth Avenue and for London Transport, as well as fashion posters for Arnold Constable and others. There is also a series of posters advertising various public parks, including Hyde Park in London.

The advertising element is usually separated from the picture, and appears in simple lettering underneath in the manner of a slogan. Some works were not intended as advertisements but had the appropriate slogans added to them later.

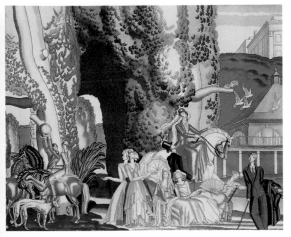

Style

Dupas' pictures are characterized by their highly individual treatment of subjects, especially women, who are very idealized and rendered in highly decorative detail. Dupas tended to dehumanize his characters, turning them into pretty, sharp-faced but sometimes expressionless mannequins. Women are always slender, willowy, demure and young, with striking features – usually high foreheads with aquiline noses, and tranquil expressions. They are always pale with rouged cheeks. The typically pure, virginal mood is often reinforced by the inclusion of white doves somewhere in the work, as in the English fashion poster in the main picture. Hair tends to be a classical 18thC type of coiffure. Colours are usually quite subdued.

Foliage is also distinctive, with exaggerated towering trees and feather-like leaves, as in the poster *above right*.

Marks

Dupas' work is always dated and signed "Jean Dupas" at the bottom of the image.

Collecting

Dupas worked in a variety of media, including watercolours, pencil and pastel on paper – which all tend to command higher prices than the posters. Oils in particular are usually very expensive. Some of the posters exist as limited edition lithographs.

The coloured lithograph *above*, from 1930, shows Dupas' distinctive treatment of architecture, with figures set in idyllic situations with simplified classical buildings with columns.
* Animals often appear in Dupas' work, and tend to be either sleek and elegant or very powerful. The horses here are typically stylized, but look powerful and monumental, with unreal features that resemble rocking or carousel horses.
* The male figures are typical elegant men-about-town, clean-shaven and complete with top hats.

LONDON TRANSPORT POSTER ARTISTS

Frank Pick, who ran London Underground during the 1920s and 30s, commissioned posters from several well-known artists in addition to Dupas, including Edward McKnight Kauffer, Frank Brangwyn, Aubrey Hammond, Rex Whistler, George Sheringham and Ashley Havinden.

The posters use bold, highly legible typefaces and bright colours. They rarely show the method of transport, and concentrate instead on the destination. Many were inducements to leisure travel, and a large proportion feature destinations in London's countryside, while others depict the attractions of central London's museums, galleries and parks. Some advertise summer and winter sales, or journeys to the theatre and cinema.

LOUIS ICART

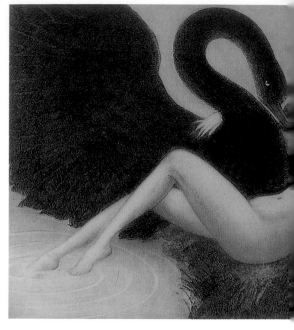

Leda and the Swan, *a Louis Icart drypoint and etching*
c.1934; 20¹/₂ x 31in/52 x79cm; value code C

Identification checklist for the work of Icart
1. Is the subject an idealized, possibly aristocratic female?
2. Is there an air of eroticism about the subject, whethe faint or explicit?
3. Are dresses and gowns feminine and flowing?
4. Are subjects engaged in "modern" activities and/or associated with speed – for example, flying or horse riding?
5. Is the composition dominated by just two or three colours or tones?
6. Is part of the work in soft focus, created by so colours and shading?

Louis Icart (French, 1850-1950)
Louis Icart trained as a printer and in the first decade of the 20thC worked for a Parisian postcard company. In 1908 he set up his own atelier, initially printing magazines and fashion leaflets. He produced a small number of works between 1911 and 1920, but his most prolific period was the 1920s and 30s. During these years he produced hundreds of lithographs and etchings, and a number of oils and gouaches.

Note
Icart's interiors are often luxurious, while many of his outdoor scenes evoke the Paris of the 1920s and 30s.

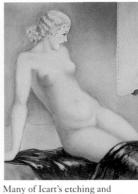

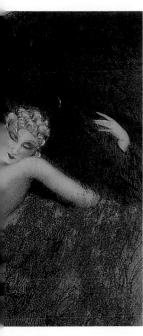

Many of Icart's etching and drypoint works are single nude or semi-nude studies, but not all of them are explicitly erotic. This one, executed in 1932, and in English entitled *My Model*, shares an air of naughtiness and exuberance with the *Attic Room* shown left, in contrast to the openly sexual *Leda and the Swan*, which appealed far more to the French market than to those of Britain and the United States.

Icart's female subjects

Icart depicted hundreds of women in his works; these are invariably the "modern", wealthy woman of 1920s and 30s Paris. Their figures are often idealized, the hair curled according to the fashion of the day, and eyeshadow usually quite prominent. When not naked, they tend to wear scant lingerie or romantic gowns.
* Animals are sometimes featured: they are often sleek and speedy and sometimes interact with the female subject in a somewhat erotic way. Horses, lions and butterflies also appear.

Colouring

Two or three colours or tones usually predominate. The soft, shaded focus of the prints on this page is characteristic. Primary colours and solid blocks are avoided.
* It is important to differentiate between the original works, which were mostly drypoint and etching executed in copperplate, and later photogravures (photographic reproductions) of the lithographs which are not collectable: the later reproductions are flat to the touch and have a lack of clarity; under close inspection their dot composition is evident (see p. 127).

Icart's works were enormously popular in America and after a visit there in 1922 he began to produce some etchings especially for distribution there. The etching and drypoint *above*, printed in colours, is signed in the lower right-hand corner "Copyright 1940 by L. Icart, Paris, New York", indicating that it was marketed in both countries.

Most works have French titles, but American galleries or distributors sometimes gave them an English name instead or as well. Sometimes the French title appears in copperplate script on the front of the work. This etching was sold under the title *Attic Room*.

ERTÉ

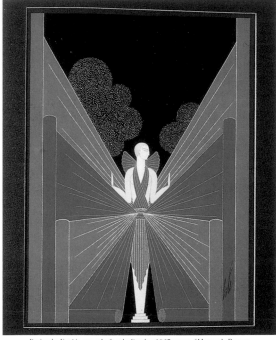

Design by Erté in gouache for the October 1927 cover of Harper's Bazaar
1927; 15 x 11¹/₂in/38 x 29cm; value code B

Identification checklist for the work of Erté
1. Is the costume futuristic or exotic, and fairly scant?
2. Are the figures idealized, with stylized faces?
3. Is there an air of sophistication and elegance to the subjects?
4. Is there a striking regard for symmetry?
5. Is the coiffure, where visible, discreet?
6. Is the work signed?
7. Is the subject pale and set against a dark background?

Collecting
Erté was a prolific designer and his work has survived in quantity. A favourite combination was gouache on paper or board, combined with gold paint, to give a jewel-like quality. The original gouaches of the 1920s and 30s are much sought-after, as are the drawings that went toward the finished design which were preserved by the artist. Original prints are also highly collectable. In the United States in recent years some of his designs have 134

been reproduced in bronze.
Erté's work is extremely well-documented, and a catalogue raisonné is also available.
Apart from its individual style, his work is recognizable by its distinct script signature, which usually appears in the corner of the work. Some designs are numbered and stamped. Many carry a wealth of information: the design *above* is signed and dated, and is stamped on the reverse "Composition Originale". It also carries the title *Robes Nouvelles*.

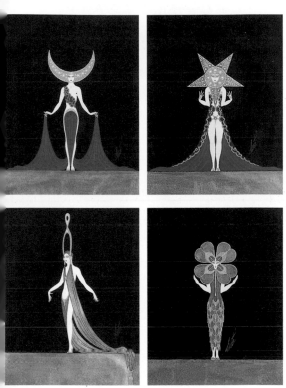

Designs for jewelry, clockwise from top left, New Moon, Lucky Star, Four Leaf Clover, *and* Wishbone *all executed in gouache and gold paint on paper.*

"Erté" – Romain de Tirtoff (Russian, 1892-1990)

Erté (the name is derived from the French pronunciation of the R and T in the artist's initials) was among the leading graphic artists, illustrators and fashion designers of his day. In addition to costumes, he designed stage sets and magazine covers. He was strongly influenced by the French music halls and by the success of the *Ballet Russes;* thus his costumes, which tend to be scant, are invariably bizarre and theatrical, often incorporating exotic headdress with feathers or motifs. Many garments have long sweeping trains. Women often wear jewelry. Hair, where visible, is usually short and not elaborately coiffured: nothing is allowed to detract from the extravagant costumes and headdress. Figures are often raised on stage-like platforms or plinths, emphasizing the theatricality of the design.

Erté also painted simpler silhouettes, and not just of women – there are a few male figures as well. Silhouettes occasionally appear as several images superimposed on each other. As well as fashion magazines such as *Vogue,* and the other leading magazines of the 20s and 30s, Erté provided the accompanying illustrations for stories that appeared in *Cosmopolitan* magazine. Between 1914/5 and 1936 he designed the covers for *Harper's Bazaar.*

La Gazette du Bon Ton

Erté was one of a number of leading illustrators who produced pochoir prints (see p. 136) for this important fashion periodical published in France between 1912 and 1925. Other contributors included Georges Lepape, Georges Barbier, André Marty, and Robert Bonfils.

GEORGES LEPAPE

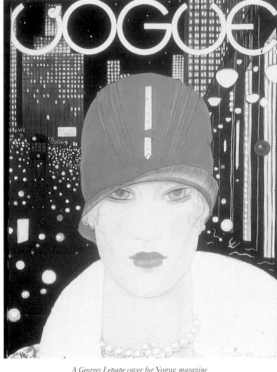

A Georges Lepape cover for Vogue *magazine
c.1927; approx 16x12in/40.5x30.5cm; value code E.*

Identification checklist for the work of Lepape
1. Is the subject a modern woman in a contemporary setting?
2. Does the main figure or subject totally dominate the composition?
3. Is there a bold use of colour to emphasize the subject?
4. Is the background simplified?
5. Is there any evidence of Japanese influence – for example, in facial expressions or the use of colour?

Pochoir prints

From the end of the 19th century in France, gouache originals, such as those by Lepape and other artists of the period, were often reproduced in the form of *pochoir* prints, using a stencil technique, made with a combination of stencils and handpainting. The result far outstripped that of machine printing and, in the hands of a skilled printer, could
136

be a very close match to the original. The prints were produced in large quantities and, as individual pages, are modestly priced. Complete issues of the magazines in which they featured are, however, rare and expensive. Some of the prints were issued separately in a larger picture size, and some of those that come on the market are still in their original frames.

Georges Lepape (French, 1887-1971)

From about 1910 Lepape's work appeared in fashion albums such as *Les Choses*; French magazines, notably *La Gazette du Bon Ton*, and his illustrations also adorned many of the covers of *Vogue* magazine in America. Other examples of his work are in the form of book illustrations, posters and advertising brochures.

In their day Lepape's illustrations would have been regarded as strikingly modern and inventive: subjects are placed in the perfect contemporary situation - for example, against skyscrapers. Women were liberated from the tame domestic environments of earlier years and allowed to make a playground of this urban city setting.

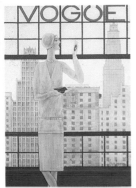

Lepape was first and foremost a fashion illustrator and this emerges in all his work. In the *Vogue* illustration *above*, of 1928, the costume interacts strikingly with the setting, the woman assuming a skyscraper figure. (Similarly, in the cover shown *opposite*, the woman's hat is lit by one of the skyscrapers.) In both cases the colours have been carefully chosen to further highlight the costumes.
* Lepape paid careful attention to detail and this can often help in dating a picture – for example, the short pearls on the lady here belong emphatically to the late twenties.

Signatures

Most of Lepape's illustrations are dated and signed with his surname, usually in a bottom corner.

GEORGE BARBIER (French, 1882-1932)

Another leading French artist, many of Barbier's illustrations are in the form of *pochoir* prints. The finest ones were produced as woodcuts by F.L. Schmied. Barbier designed fashion plates and posters and illustrations for books.

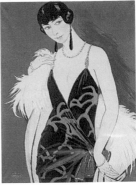

Barbier's women are generally fuller figured and more sensual than those of Lepape. The background is extremely subtle if not actually totally plain, as here. As a fashion illustrator, his approach could be daring: in this 1922 gouache, *Elegante en robe du soir bleue* he shows only part of the evening dress being advertised.

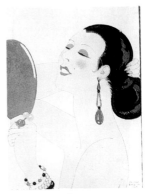

Barbier's style shows a strong Japanese influence exemplified here in *Le miroir rouge* of 1923 by the use of flat blocks of colour and an Oriental-looking subject.
* Characteristically, the work is signed and dated in the bottom right-hand corner.

ERNST DRYDEN

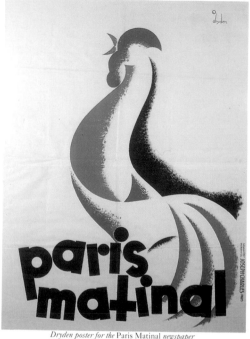

Dryden poster for the Paris Matinal *newspaper c.1928; ht 61x43in/155x108.5cm; value code C*

Identification checklist for the work of Ernst Dryden
1. Does the subject stand out strongly against a plain or smaller-scale background, perhaps with clever use of persepctive?
2. Is the work signed?
3. Does the work conjure up an air of stylish, relaxed, modern elegance?
4. Is there a sensitive use of colour, perhaps restricted to just two tones, or a palette of a few subtle complementary colours?
5. Is any lettering integrated with the design in an elegant or inventive way?
6. Does the design convey its message clearly and boldly, perhaps with an element of wit?

Ernst Dryden (Austrian, 1883-1938)
Dryden was born Ernst Deutsch, and changed his name in 1919. He was a pupil of Gustav Klimt, and became a prominent illustrator and costume designer. From 1926 he designed covers for the Parisian fashion magazine *Die*

Dame, of which he was art director, as well as designing advertisements for a range of international clients, including Persil, Bugatti and Cinzano. In 1933 Dryden moved to Hollywood, where he designed sets and costumes for many major films.

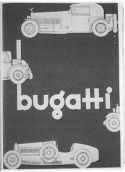

Dryden's clever use of restrained colours and his imaginative integration of the picture and lettering are clearly seen in this 1927 advertisement. The combination of the relaxed and the dramatic is typical.

Collecting Dryden

Very little of Dryden's work had appeared on the market before 1976, when 4000 drawings, sketches and posters were discovered. This has led to a reassessment of his work and prices are rising accordingly. The earlier works with the Deutsch signature, are easier to find than those from 1919 on, which are signed "Dryden" or "dryden" with a small circular eye over the "d". The original artwork appears on the market from time to time, but is more expensive than the posters.

GORDON CONWAY
(American, 1894-1956)
Another stylish and versatile illustrator, Gordon Conway did her first work for *Vanity Fair* in New York. From 1920 to 1934 she worked in London for *The Tatler* and other magazines, as well as designing for revues, Paris plays and a number of British films. In 1934 she returned to the U.S.

Like Dryden, Conway has been recently rediscovered, and prices for her work are likely to rise.

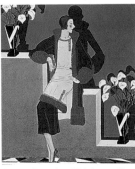

Conway's work, which is usually signed with her full name, is instantly recognizable for its use of bold, contrasting colours, stylized figures and two-dimensional design elements – all features of this poster from c.1925. Much of her work reveals the influence of Lepape and Barbier (see pp. 136-7).

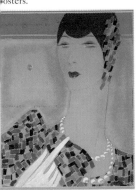

The background is totally subjugated to the female subject in this unfinished artwork for a poster, 1928, advertising Farben paints. The lady is typically chic, with idealized features.

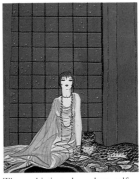

The sophisticated, modern, self-possessed subject of *Woman With Leopard* (1924) is typical of Conway's women, who, with their geometric hairstyles, stylized faces and cool poses, epitomize the jazz age. Her works often incorporate exotic elements.

139

MINOR PRINTS AND POSTERS

Loose fashion plates and contemporary magazines with colour illustrations probably provide the best opportunity for putting together a collection of graphics at a very low cost. Many are well-executed and attractive but suffer in value because they are by an unknown or little known artist. There is also growing interest in other printed ephemera such as cigarette cards, illustrated sheet music and chocolate box covers. Avoid pictures that have been pasted on board as this renders them almost valueless: ideally, they should be unmounted or at least mounted professionally, using acid-free boards.

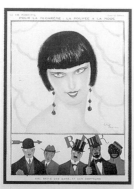 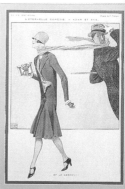

These two plates are from the French magazine, *La Vie Parisienne*. The example on the *left* shows a typically idealized woman of the time, with dark bobbed hair, an orientalized expression and pendant earrings. However, it lacks the depth and definition of work by leading French artists. Many of the most charming graphics of the period are those with an element of humour, such as that on the *right*, entitled *The Eternal Comedy – Adam and Eve ... and the serpent*, which uses the scarf to make a play on words.

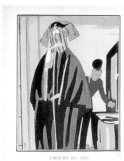 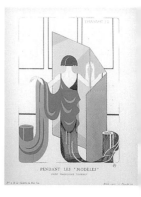

These two prints, also by lesser-known artists, are both from the *Gazette du Bon Ton*. The one on the *left* is typical of the period in its use of perspective for dramatic effect: the model's exaggerated height adds to her glamour. In the well-balanced composition on the right, the fabrics being advertised stand out from a simple, modern background.

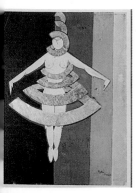
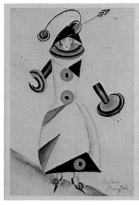

These two small pictures (less than 12in/30cm) from c.1925 by Lydia Mandel, an obscure artist, are in gouache, but the colours have faded slightly. Strongly Cubist influences can be seen in the stylized, geometric shapes.

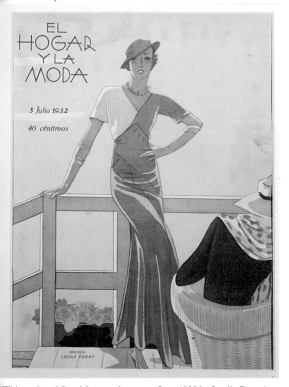

This unsigned Spanish magazine cover from 1932 by Lucile Paray is of fine quality and interesting design, but is reduced in value by water staining. The colours have retained their clarity, and there is no evidence of tears, although these may be hidden by the mount.

141

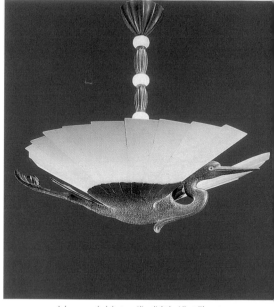

A bronze and alabaster ceiling light by Albert Cheuret

The 1920s and 30s witnessed a new interest in wrought iron as a decorative and functional medium: decorative as a surround for blown vases; functional for items such as gates, screens and radiator covers.

The period saw a revival of the craftsman-metalworkers, the most famous of whom were the Frenchmen Edgar Brandt (who later moved to the United States), Paul Kiss and Louis Majorelle. They often worked in conjunction with other manufacturers – for example, Majorelle made mounts for glass produced by Daum. Metalwork was taken to its high point in France by Armand Albert Rateau, who developed exotic bronze furniture cast in a highly individualistic style – for example, a bronze and marble table is supported by four stylized pheasants.

At the other extreme, the market was catered for by the creations of the German firm WMF, which has been successful with Art Nouveau and Classical art pewter, but now concentrated on relatively simple forms, often with geometric simulated bronze patination and silvering.

Metal was put to a variety of new uses, especially in France. Several manufacturers used wrought and hammered ironwork as mounts for light fixtures, especially for ceilings. Edgar Brandt made cobra standard lamps (with Daum glass shades) that showed innovative use of bronze as a lighting medium (see p.145). Screens were made in metal, often with animal motifs showing creatures popular during the period, such as snakes, gazelles and panthers. The designer Raymond Subes promoted the use of cast iron allied with plate glass for tables. Some work by Brandt was incorporated into the fittings of Selfridges department store in London. Much of his work was produced to commission for important New York buildings (see pp. 144-5).

Dinanderie, the application of patinated enamel to non-precious metals such as copper and steel, was taken to its peak by Claudius Linossier and Jean Dunand. The use of spelter was still widespread; it was employed to a large extent in sculpture, and in some instances during the 1920s for car mascots in chromed metal, made by a number of artists. Many car mascots, especially in the United States, were made for specific models of cars, and are now very collectable.

In Britain very little of significance was produced. Some work was designed for Liberty, especially the range of simulated hammered "Tudric" pewter, adapted from the firm's earlier Art Nouveau designs in pewter. Although these used simple forms they nevertheless seemed almost a token effort to modernize the range. Other pewter manufacturers used Cubistic forms in an attempt to maintain the momentum of growth in the art pewter industry. Scandinavia produced some very Classical metalwork.

American artists were initially influenced by French metalworkers, but soon began to develop their own styles, working in stainless steel and aluminium on a large scale, and were particularly fond of chrome, using it extensively in interiors and for furniture, friezes, and elevator doors. The International Copper Company patented a nickel-copper alloy called "Monel" metal, as a popular alternative to aluminium.

Not all metalwork was made to private commission or for the exclusive end of the market: it is still possible to find relatively inexpensive pieces today, such as kitchenware and other small household items, especially if they are anonymous or not attributed to major craftsmen.

Condition is important, although rust on ironwork is not a cause for concern: it can be stripped, treated with anti-rust agent and then repainted with metal paint, as long as the work is done sympathetically. However, some vases have had their patination polished off, and these are thus rendered valueless. Most pieces are signed with a stamp. As yet, very little has been faked or reproduced.

Medallions (small plaques) are one neglected area collectors may find worth pursuing. They tend to be underrated, perhaps because they are neither functional nor do they lend themselves well to display, and they are therefore still modestly priced. Many are commemorative, and include the work of top French sculptors, some of whom, such as Paul Turin and Jean Vernon, specialized in this area. The classic example is the medal produced for the 1925 Exhibition in Paris (see p. 9). Medals are often signed and usually cast in bronze. The condition is very important: dents, scratches and over-polishing render them near worthless.

EDGAR BRANDT

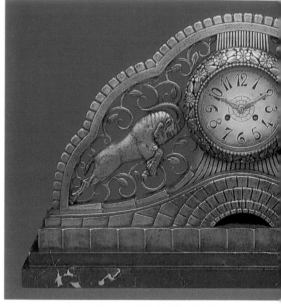

A silvered bronze mantel clock by Edgar Brandt
c.1925; ht 15¹/₂in/39.5cm; wdth 25¹/₂in/65cm; value code B

Identification checklist for the metalwork of Edgar Brandt
1. Is the piece partly or entirely composed of wrought iron, or of cast or silvered bronze?
2. Do the surfaces have a textured appearance?
3. Are the joints and any screws or bolts subtle, or even concealed?
4. Does the piece have ornate decorative elements, such as scrolls or overlapping flowerheads?
5. Does the symmetry of the piece seem natural rather than mechanical and rigid?
6. Is the piece stamped "E. Brandt", probably on the footrim?
7. Does an animal form part of the subject?

Edgar Brandt (French, 1880-1960)
Brandt began working in iron at an early age. He made mostly jewelry and wrought-iron work until 1919, when he opened his own atelier in Paris, producing his own designs and those of other designers. His work was acclaimed in 1925, when he co-designed the Porte d'Honneur for the Paris Exhibition, and exhibited his famous five-panel, wrought iron and brass screen, Oasis. With its stylized central fountain and French Art Deco-type scrolls, the screen was typical of much of the work Brandt produced during the 1920s. The warm patination and the combination of iron, brass, copper and other metals were typical.

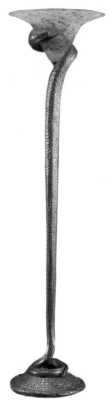

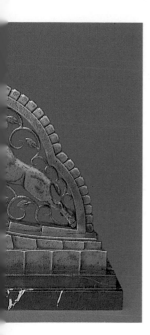

Wares and styles

Brandt was the leading metalworker of the period both in Paris and New York, where he opened Ferrobrandt Inc., a company that executed commissions for a number of buildings, and also produced a range of domestic wares.

He used the decorative elements of wrought iron to great effect, popularizing the hammered *martelé* finish. Although other metalworkers emulated him, Brandt's work remained technically supreme. In his hands a material of structural purpose became highly decorative, with superbly executed spirals, scrolls and animals.

As well as industrial commissions, such as railings, grilles and so on, Brandt produced a range of highly collectable domestic items. These include:
* radiator covers
* screens
* umbrella stands
* centre tables
* fireplace accessories.

He also made small decorative wares such as jewelry, trays, vases and paper knives.

Brandt is probably best known for his bronze serpent lamp, *La Tentation*, made as a table lamp, a standard lamp and in an intermediate size. The glass shade was by Daum. Fakes abound. These can usually be detected by the poor quality of the patination; by the lack of definition in the casting of the snake; and by the shades, which are usually of lightweight glass, inferior in quality to the Daum originals. On an original lamp the shade and support meet perfectly; the shade and support of a fake are a poor fit and do not make contact. Before making a purchase compare the article with one known to be genuine. Beware of lamps with old wirings and fixtures, as these may have been taken from another old lamp to create an impression of age. Similarly, a perfectly genuine old lamp may well have new wires and fixtures.

RAYMOND SUBES

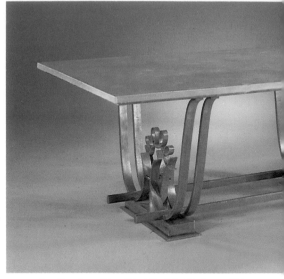

A marble and wrought iron dining table attributed to Raymond Subes c.1928; ht 29^1/$_2$in/75cm, wdth 79in/200cm; value code A

Identification checklist for the metalwork of Subes
1. Is the piece wrought iron, possibly gilded?
2. Are there floral motifs, possibly stylized?
3. Is any decoration integral with the form?
4. Is the form relatively heavy and durable?
5. Does the piece have a complex form of support?
6. If the form is a table, does it have a large rectangular marble or granite top?

Raymond Subes (French, 1893-1970)
Next to Brandt (see pp. 144-5), Subes is probably the most renowned French metalworker of the Deco period. In 1919 he became director of the metal workshop of Borderel and Robert, a major architectural construction company. Most of his work was on government commissions, notably the *Normandie* (see p. 9) and other important liners of the period, to which he contributed wall decorations, as well as gilded metalwork. Like Brandt, Subes initially worked mainly in wrought iron, and occasionally in bronze and copper. By the 1930s his medium had changed to
aluminium and oxydized or lacquered steel.

Form and decoration
Subes' output was prodigious: despite their hand-finished look, his tables, mirrors, lamps and radiator cases were mainly mass-produced using industrial methods. His early motifs tend toward the naturalistic and slightly florid. Iron was finely bent into ribbon-or octopus-like curls, often curving away from a central source. By the end of the 1920s, decoration had become minimal and was often restricted to the supports – for example, the S-shaped straps of the table *above*.

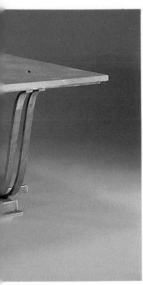

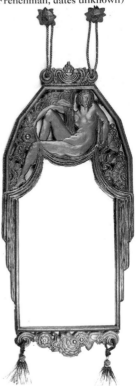

PAUL KISS (Rumanian born, became naturalized Frenchman, dates unknown)

Later style
During the 1930s Subes' work became much heavier in appearance – a factor which helps to distinguish his work from that of Brandt. Pieces are often of bronze or aluminium, and employ architectural shapes: fluted columns and fans, rectangular stepped or panelled plinths, and so on. Forms are simple and bold. His large 1930s light reflectors, which throw light onto the ceiling, were innovative and striking. The impression given by all of Subes' pieces in this period is of massive size and strength.

Beware
Much of Subes' work is difficult to identify as it is incorporated into fixtures, such as building façades, balustrades, door frames, furniture mounts, and so on. Subes pieces coming onto the market are still rarities, and often unsigned.

Other iron-workers
The late 1920s and 30s were the culmination of the iron-work revival. Other designers working in wrought-iron at the time were Jules and Michel Nics, known as Nics Frères. They specialized in martelé (hammered or planished) surfaces, hand-made furniture and decorative wares.

Kiss was another important metalworker of the period working in France at the same time as Subes. Like Brandt (see pp.114-15), he preferred ornate designs and motifs and his work displays keen attention to detail.

As well as wrought iron, Kiss worked in silvered bronze. He is particularly known for his mirrors, which tend to have an elongated form and may include decorative tassels; some are supported by silk cords, like the example *above*, which also shows his tendency to use a reeded effect or other device to give the metal a textured look. Pieces are often mounted or set off by marble, alabaster or engraved glass. He also made console and mirror sets, table lamps, and ceiling fixtures.

Kiss's work usually has a stamped signature "P. KISS PARIS" or "P. KISS".

CLAUDIUS LINOSSIER

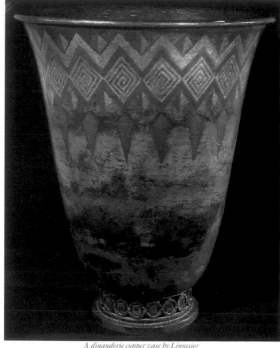

*A dinanderie copper vase by Linossier
1920s; ht 15^1/2in/39.5cm; value code C*

Identification checklist for Linossier metalwork
1. Is the piece metal?
2. Are the colours muted and autumnal?
3. Does the pattern contain geometric motifs?
4. Is the piece obviously handmade?
5. Is the surface textured, patinated or inlaid?
6. Is the object seamless?
7. Does it bear Linossier's stamped signature?
8. Is the form tall and elegant?
9. Does the shape taper toward the base?
10. If the decoration is not all over, is it concentrated mostly at the top?
11. Is the footrim narrow, perhaps latticed?
12. Do everted shapes have a turnover, or lipped, rim?

Signatures
Most pieces are stamped "Cl. Linossier", in the bottom right-hand corner on the footrim. Some are dated as well. The wares have been copied but not faked (see facing page).
148

Recognition point
The narrow interlaced footrim of this vase is characteristic of Linossier, as is the combination of geometric banding in materials that stand out against the degraded metallic patination.

Claudius Linossier (French, 1893-1955)

Linossier is chiefly noted for the elegant design and textured surfaces of his vases, bowls and plates, produced by his workshop in Lyon. He worked in copper, brass and occasionally silver. Surfaces retain the hammered texture, and are often chased, encrusted in metal (often silver) that contrasts with the patinated background, or inlaid with fired designs in which adjacent metals are finely fused. Surfaces are often patinated in black and russet, or dappled polychrome.

Dinanderie

The technique of dinanderie (work in non-precious metals) reached a peak of popularity in the 1920s and early 1930s. Linossier was apprenticed to its foremost exponent, Jean Dunand (see pp. 18-19) and his geometric, deliberately primitive designs, produced during the 1920s, reveal Dunand's influence. Dinanderie work has a handmade look that is difficult to reproduce by machine: pieces are usually taken from a single, seamless sheet of copper to which inlays such as silver and various alloys are added.

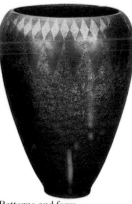

Patterns and form

As well as an inverted bell shape, Linossier also used a baluster form, like that shown *above*. The bands of diamonds and chevrons are also characteristic, as is their position – near the top of the piece and pendant from the rim. Spiral motifs sometimes appear, especially on more rounded or pumpkin-shaped forms.

WMF METALWORK

Linossier's work was emulated by WMF, who used a mass-produced technique of applying metallic deposits to their vases in various colours. The vases were mass-produced by an electrolytic process, and were made up of seamed pieces. Surfaces were not textured but patinated, which gives a slightly rigid appearance. Although less desirable than Linossier's, WMF wares are nevertheless collectable.

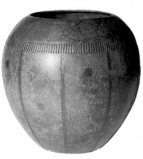

WMF wares are usually smaller than Linoissier's; this vase is 8in/20.5 cm high. Although clearly not hand-made, it is nevertheless well-proportioned and has an attractive finish – and is likely to be within the budget of most collectors.
* A number of highly polished examples have appeared on the market, the patination having been stripped, often out of ignorance. These vases should be avoided.

The WMF mark is distinctive, and is not known to have been faked.

GANTCHEFF (French, active 1920s)

Another French firm, Gantcheff, made dinanderie wares in Paris in the 1920s. These compare with those made by Linossier for quality and attractiveness and although less well known in England and the United States, tend to fetch similar prices to Linossier's work. Wares are usually signed on the footrim.

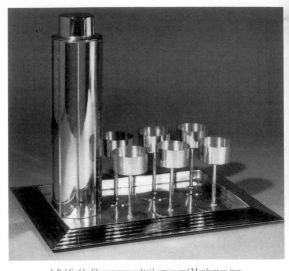

A Bel Geddes Skyscraper cocktail service and Manhattan tray 1937; ht of shaker 12³/₄in/32.4cm; wdth of tray 15¹/₄in/38.4cm; value code D

Identification checklist for the work of Bel Geddes

1. Does the design show futuristic elements?
2. Is the design very streamlined?
3. Are there discernible signs of the influence of industrial design?
4. Are the materials and methods of manufacture representative of a "Machine Age"?

Norman Bel Geddes
(American, 1893-1958)

Bel Geddes was prominent among a group of talented and highly qualified designers, notably Russel Wright, Raymond Loewy, Henry Dreyfuss and Walter Dorwin Teague, who were drawn to industrial design for its artistic and creative potential. Bel Geddes trained as a theatre and set designer before setting himself up as an industrial designer in 1927. His early commissions, before 1932, were for domestic products, such as gas stoves.

He produced designs for a wide variety of American corporations, such as IBM and General Motors. He also designed furniture, including some for the Simmons Co., which celebrated metal, rather than attempting to use metal to simulate wood.

150

Bel Geddes can be largely credited with creating the streamlined style, which replaced the sharp angles of the 1920s with smooth, sleek rounded forms suggestive of energy and movement. It was a style which was to permeate both interiors and exteriors of buildings, and which proved to be perhaps the most evident form of Art Deco in the United States. He declared it treatment suitable for virtually any product, and although some of his more outlandish suggestions for futuristic steam locomotives, transatlantic airliners and so on were not realized, he did produce designs for airplane interiors in the streamlined style. His approach to industrial design followed closely the principles of the Bauhaus (see pp. 142-3) in the attempt to integrate form with function.

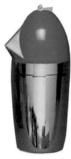

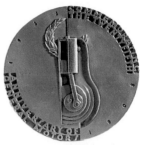

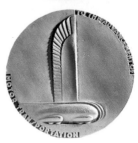

Some small streamlined wares were very successful – for example, this chromed-metal soda bottle with a brightly coloured cover and a chromed metal conical body, was produced in great numbers by the Walter Kidd Sales Co. Inc., who patented the design. They were made in a number of different colours and were originally sold at very low prices. They are of limited interest to collectors today, but may become more popular.

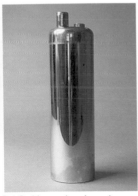

Bel Geddes produced metalware for several manufacturers, mostly functional designs, some of which are marked with his facsimile signature. This cocktail shaker, like the cocktail service and the serving tray shown in the main picture, is in chromium-plated metal and was commissioned by the Revere Copper and Brass Company in 1935. Typically of Bel Geddes metalware, it shows a restrained, linear style that complements the streamlined and "Skyscraper" styles of the 1930s American Art Deco.

* Cocktail wares were popular throughout the 1930s.

This commemorative medallion in silver-plated bronze was created for the 25th anniversary of General Motors in 1933. It has a moulded signature "NORMAN BEL GEDDES" and is stamped "Metallic Art Co NY". It is 3in (7.5cm) in diameter. The lettering is in a futuristic typeface that complements the Modernist image of a piston and flywheel, *above, top*, suggestive of speed and power. The reverse side of the medallion (*above, bottom*) shows a sleek highly stylized car.

WALTER DORWIN TEAGUE (American, 1883-1960)

Another primarily industrial designer, Teague is mainly remembered for the service stations he designed for Texaco in the United States in the mid-30s. He was retained by the camera company Kodak for about 30 years to design some of their cameras and packaging. He also did a number of successful designs for the glassworks of Steuben (see pp. 60-61). His work in all these media is characterized by a readiness to harmonize function with bold design. In his metalwares he often contrasted chrome metal with black lacquered metal on a streamlined form. He also used new materials: lamps were made of aluminium and plastic.

151

MINOR METALWORK

Objects in this category fall into three main areas. The first is novelty items, such as lamps in the form of boats and electrical fixtures in unusual forms. Then come items in the style of top Parisian metalworkers, such as the brooch shown *right*, which emulates the work of Edgar Brandt. Many Brandt-inspired wares are now collectable in their own right. The third area comprises objects made in chrome, which came into its own during this period; there are also many chromed and black-lacquered streamlined wares, some in novelty forms – for example, combined timepieces and lighters. Chromed metal fixtures were a feature put to great use by Odeon cinemas in Britain, both for interiors and for small accoutrements such as lighters and radios. Architectural fixtures, especially those in chrome, tend to surface with great regularity in street markets in England and elsewhere. The plating of these is often worn or flaking, but can be restored.

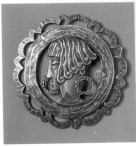

This anonymous brooch, fashioned in the manner of Edgar Brandt, is an archetypal Art Deco piece in that it uses bronze with steel or hammered ironwork and shows a typically stylized woman of the period, with bobbed hair in ringlets, and an elongated face. The earrings impart an African flavour, and suggest a date for the piece of c.1930. The back will be plain-cast. The quality of casting is quite good, but the lack of a signature means that this piece will not command a very high price.

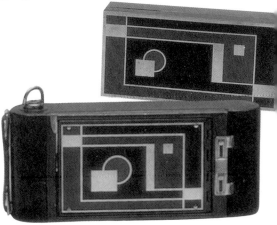

Cameras increased in popularity through the 1920s. The folding camera was a relatively new item in 1930. This example, designed for Kodak by Walter Dorwin Teague in 1930, demonstrates the application of modern geometric design to a functional object. The decoration manages to be sympathetic to the form: the function is not immediately apparent. Cameras from the 1930s are often still in perfect working order, but even if they are not, are sought-after to some extent for their decorative value. This is a fine example of an Art Deco camera, especially as it retains its original box, which echoes the design. This is rare. Without the box the camera itself would be worth 30percent less.

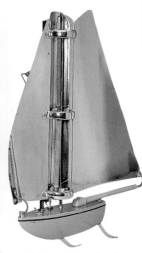

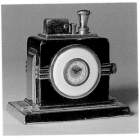

This 2½ft (75cm) high boat is an ingeniously designed electric heater: the element is in the mast, and the metal sails act as radiators. Electric heaters were a relatively new phenomenon in the 1930s, and only a few have so far appeared on the market. It is preferable, but not essential, that they be in working order.

Table lighters are probably the area that offers the greatest scope for collectors today, as there are plenty of chromed, lacquered, streamlined examples available. Many of these were a feature of fashionable homes and public buildings of the 1930s, especially in the United States. Pieces favour strong primary colours, often with contrasting appliqués in either silvered or gilt metal. This example incorporates a clock.
* Radios were also treated as both functional and decorative items during this period, and were often highly stylized. Many were produced in bakelite. Some were by top designers, including the British industrial designer Wells Coates.

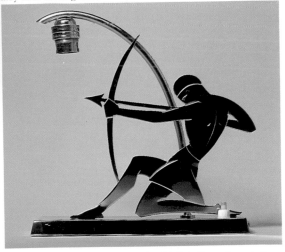

The two-dimensional figure supporting this light fixture is made from cut-out chromed sheet metal. It is highly stylized, and shows the inspiration of the amazonian images popular during the period. It is not signed. Items such as this were mass-produced, but have not so far appeared on the market in any quantity: as period pieces, they are likely to become increasingly collectable.

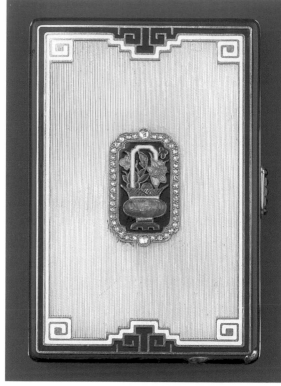

A jewelled and enamelled lady's powder compact attributed to Van Cleef and Arpels

The most important items of silver produced during this period were tablewares. The emphasis was on form, which tended to be streamlined; decoration took second place or was absent altogether.

The foremost designers were the French, most notably Jean Puiforcat, who dominated the field. The Scandinavians, the most famous of whom was Georg Jensen, produced organic, decorated forms, as did the Wiener Werkstätte in Austria. The work of Bauhaus designers, many of whom moved to the United States, was extremely influential. Marianne Brandt, who followed minimalist principles, was regarded by many as the most important Bauhaus silversmith. American designers also produced some significant work – for example the cocktail service by Norman Bel Geddes (see p. 150), which exemplifies the use of simple perpendicular forms, inspired by the skyscraper.

British designers were slow to adopt the new style, and most British silver produced during this period is traditional and undistinguished. Some silversmiths attempted to adopt new ideas, creating engine-turned geometric designs, especially for such items as cigar boxes and pocket cigarette cases. During the 1920s some British silver was still hand-made by one or two surviving guilds in Britain, including the Artificer's Guild formed by Edward Spencer. Spencer also made copper and silver caddies, boxes and other items. Otherwise, British silverware from this period was mass-produced. The firm of Whakeley & Wheeler was responsible for many of the more interesting examples.

There are a few silver trophies from this period, some of them figural. One of the most famous is by Phoebe Stabler and depicts a figure of Mercury riding on lightning. Clocks from this period exhibit a more Modernist sculptural quality than hitherto, and are in a huge variety of forms.

Guilloche enamel decoration using translucent enamels was especially popular. It was often the only decoration applied to dressing table sets, which tended to be engine-turned designs in silver covered with translucent monochrome enamel.

All silver should be hallmarked. The date, maker and provenance of a piece can be checked by referring to one of the catalogues of marks available. Occasionally the letter F is added to a British hallmark, indiciating that the piece is a foreign import which has met the British silver standard.

The luxury end of the jewelry trade was well catered for by all the major manufacturers, among them Cartier, Gerard Sandoz, and Georges Fouquet, who all used Modernist forms, although they also continued to produce pieces in more traditional styles. Exotic jewels were often incorporated, sometimes applied to novelty forms. Chinoiserie was popular, especially in the 1920s, and coral and jade, often carved, became fashionable on a scale not seen before. Glass jewelry was promoted by Lalique: the fragility of the medium means that it is now rather scarce and therefore sought after.

At the other extreme, there was a large amount of mass-produced costume dress jewelry and metalwork: techniques were evolved to simulate crushed eggshell, and some designs were painted on base metal in an attempt to simulate enamel inlay on more precious metal. These designs also made use of the new plastics. Diamanté and marcasite were frequently used, especially in sunbursts or fountain motifs.

Changes in fashion in the 1920s and 30s demanded new forms of jewelry – for example, earrings became longer as women wore their hair shorter. Brooches became very popular, and were worn on outdoor clothing, especially coat collars, not just on evening wear as before. The lady's wristwatch proved popular in the 1920s and 30s, the best examples being French. Watch faces were often silver or platinum inset with geometric initials or paste stones. Utility items, such as powder compacts, cigarette cases, evening bags and clasps for bags were popular, and there was still a strong market for enamelled dressing table sets.

JEAN PUIFORCAT

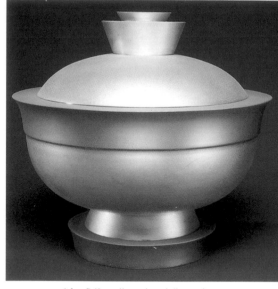

*A Jean Puiforcat silver and parcel-gilt covered tureen
c.1935; ht 9in/24 cm; value code C*

Identification checklist for Puiforcat silver
1. Is the form simplified and rounded?
2. Is the surface plain and smooth?
3. Is the piece strongly functional, showing a Cubist influence?
4. Does the piece bear a French hallmark and the signature "Jean E. Puiforcat"?
5. Does the piece use materials other than silver on handles or knobs?

Jean Puiforcat (French, 1897-1945)

Puiforcat joined the successful family firm after the First World War. He concentrated on graceful shapes and rejected traditional embellishments without sacrificing either beauty or luxury. Surfaces are usually left plain. Even the hammer marks – traditionally the sign of a hand-made object – are absent. Instead, the surface is enlivened by the way in which the large, perfectly smooth areas catch, reflect and distort light. All Puiforcat pieces show a very high standard of craftmanship and minute attention to detail. Straightforward silversmithing techniques are used.

156

1920s style

Puiforcat made functional rather than decorative pieces. In the 1920s he produced tea sets, dishes and bowls in solid silver in simple cylindrical or rectangular forms. These are offset by knobs and handles of ivory, jade, lapis lazuli or hardwood.

1930s style

In the 1930s Puiforcat's style gave way to purer, sleeker shapes which are bold statements of form and volume, with occasional touches of ice-green or salmon-pink glass, high-quality wood or crystal. These later objects sometimes appear futuristic, a style exemplified by the tureen *above*.

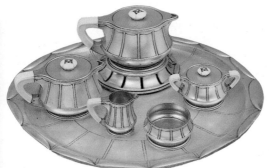

Puiforcat tea and coffee sets were mass-produced and survive in large numbers. Many have ivory knobs and handles, as does this tea service from c.1930. While the handles are primarily functional, acting as insulators, they are often the only decorative elements in a piece. This service is unusually ornate – for example, the banding around the bases is of amber bakelite. The tray is an integral part of the set, and has decorative ribbing and scalloped borders to match.

CHRISTOFLE (French, 1839-present)

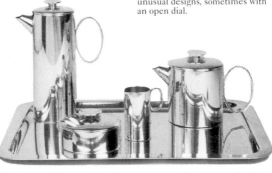

Although it had been cautious in its use of the Art Nouveau style, this family firm was more receptive than Puiforcat to the simplicity and geometricism of Art Deco. The firm produced all kinds of utilitarian and decorative silverplate. In the 1920s they commissioned pieces from a number of notable designers, including Gio Ponti, Maurice Daurat, Luc Lanel, Süe et Mare, Paul Follot and Christian Fjerdingstad. Pieces were mass-produced, many in electroplate, a

* Some wares, although functioning perfectly as coffee pots or jugs, also appear as pieces of abstract, Cubist sculpture.
* Incomplete tea and coffee sets suffer a disproportionate drop in value, and are probably not worth collecting at all unless very inexpensive.

Marks
All Puiforcat pieces are stamped "Puiforcat" on the base and carry a French hallmark.

Clocks
Puiforcat also made silver clocks in this period. These often have unusual designs, sometimes with an open dial.

process perfected by the firm in the mid-19thC. This was used for tableware, including some for the *Normandie* and other liners. This five-piece tea and coffee service designed by Henri Bouilhet in c.1925 has typically clean and geometric shapes, with spindly handles. The surfaces are plain; decoration, when present, is usually incorporated in the plating.
* The bases of pieces are stamped "Christofle" and indicate the grade of silver used.

157

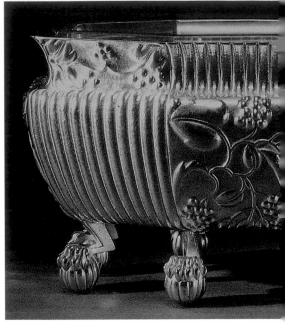

A silver Wiener Werkstätte centrepiece
c.1920; lgth 10in/25.4cm; value code B

Identification checklist for the work of Dagobert Pêche, a prominent Wiener Werkstätte silversmith of the period
1. Does the design have a strong organic element, possibly incorporating heart-shaped leaves and berries?
2. Is the piece fairly heavily decorated for the period, with few plain surfaces?
3. Is it hand-made?
4. Is the base marked with a monogrammed "P" (for pieces by Pêche) and the "WW" monogram?
5. Does the design incorporate planished (hand-beaten) decoration?

Wiener Werkstätte (Austrian, 1903-32)
This group of artisans worked in a number of different media and styles, which makes it difficult to generalize about their work. It aimed to provide a commercial enterprise, uniting artists with craftsmen, to create everyday items incorporating the ideals of the decorative arts. The organization was committed to functionalism and expressionism, and even before 1914 its artists were creating severe, unornamented pieces, which later found expression under the banner of Art Deco. Thus, many of the Wiener Werkstätte pieces traditionally associated with the Art Deco style were in fact made before the 1920s. After the First World War a more spontaneous style developed, and by the late 20s/early 30s pieces tend towards an ornamented, more decorative style, especially those by Dagobert Pêche (see *facing page*).

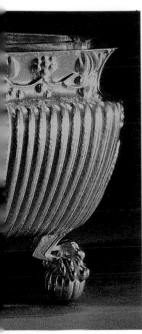

Dagobert Pêche (Austrian, 1887-1923)

Pêche was a designer working in all fields of the decorative arts, including furniture, ceramics, glass, bookbinding, textiles and wallpapers. In 1915 he joined the Wiener Werkstätte. His work has a strong organic emphasis, seen clearly in the silver centrepiece *above*. Work is relatively ornate compared with other silverware of the 1920s and 30s and surfaces are very seldom plain: the decorated centre panel of berried plants with large, heart-shaped leaves is typical. Pêche also liked to use flowering plant motifs. The eight strangely angular claw supports are reminiscent of traditional claw-and-ball feet, but the style is highly individual, with each claw grasping a fluted melon ball. The fluted panels are typical of much Wiener Werkstätte work, and can be found on pieces in other metals as well as silver. Like Georg Jensen, Pêche also liked to use ivory in his silverware.

Pêche's work is usually stamped with an elongated "P" mark and the Wiener Werkstätte monogram.

Silver

Much Wiener Werkstätte silverwork was made on a commission basis, so many pieces are one-offs. They were all hand-made in the manner used by 18thC silversmiths – in contrast to Britain and the United States, where mass-production techniques were introduced during this period. Shapes borrowed from 18thC silver were very much in vogue during this period; avant-garde pieces were made in relatively small quantities.

Marks

The rose mark was registered as a trademark in 1903, probably the same year that the Wiener Werkstätte monogram within an oval was registered as a hallmark. The name "Wiener Werkstätte" was registered as a trademark in 1913 and the "WW" monogram in 1914. The individual artists and craftsmen of the group all have their own monograms, but care must be exercised in attributing work to specific craftsmen, as the form and decoration were not necessarily designed by the same person. The organization occasionally also issued licenses, allowing its designs to be executed in other workshops. Works all carry serial numbers, but these are unreliable as a means of dating as they were sometimes changed, also, a number of copies were made of some designs, often with slight variations. However, pieces are sometimes dated.

Josef Hoffman (Austrian, 1870-1956)

Hoffman was one of the founder members of the Wiener Werkstätte. Although much of his work is in the severe style of the early 19thC, Hoffman continued to produce pieces for the Wiener Werkstätte until the 1930s. His silverwork is characterized by its use of smooth metal surfaces. He also designed jewelry, glassware and furniture. His work is rarely as ornate as that of Pêche, but often uses original and interesting shapes for conventional objects, such as cutlery. He had a strong preference for cube- or square-shaped decoration and for chequered effects.

159

GEORG JENSEN

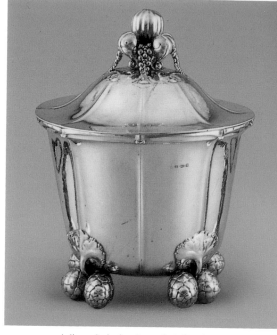

A silver caviar bowl on pine cone feet by Georg Jensen 1930; ht 14in/35.5cm; value code C

Identification checklist for Jensen silver
1. Is the surface fairly plain, without engraving or other decoration?
2. Are highlights (knops, feet and so on) comparatively ornate?
3. Is the item high quality and obviously intended for a luxury market?
4. Is there a suggestion of Art Nouveau-style organic motifs, such as pods and tendrils?
5. Does the form exhibit a Neo-classical influence?
6. Is the piece marked?
7. Does it have a highly polished finish?

Georg Jensen, (Danish, 1866-1935)
From 1880 Jensen worked as a goldsmith in Copenhagen, gradually moving into silverwork. He opened his first shop in 1904 and soon had branches in Paris, London, New York and other major cities. Together with his partner Johan Rohde, he designed much of the firm's output but also

employed several artists, notably Harald Nielsen from 1909 and, in the 1930s, Sigvard Bernadotte; the latter was responsible for many of the firm's linear incised engraved bodies. The Jensen workshops made tea and coffee sets, candlesticks, cocktail shakers, tureens, cigar boxes, jewelry and other, often modern or luxury items.

Decorative styles

Jensen's silver has some affinities with Arts and Crafts and Art Nouveau work, especially in its use of organic, pod and tendril motifs and shapes. Elements are also borrowed from Neo-classicism and from nature, combining to create a highly individual look that pioneered the Art Deco style in silver. Ornamentation tends to be restricted to features such as knops, feet and handles. The main body is seldom embellished – the emphasis is almost entirely on form, as is the case with this cocktail shaker, *right*. Geometric forms and motifs are stringently avoided. Inset semi-precious stones are sometimes used.

Marks

Jensen pieces bear a variety of marks – usually, the guarantee of silver, the Jensen manufactory mark and maker's initials, and a shape number. Some pieces bear an importer's mark enabling them to be sold as silver outside Denmark. In Britain, pieces that do not bear this mark are designated "silver-coloured". The caviar bowl is marked "Georg Jensen 925 S no.87"

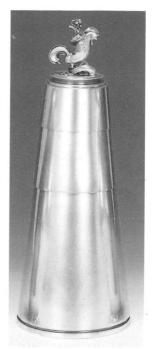

MARCEL WOLFERS
(French, dates unknown)

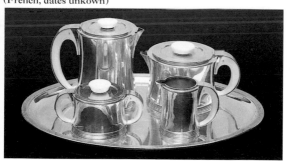

Like Jensen, Marcel Wolfers concentrated on luxury items with simple, solid forms and spare decoration. The decorative elements of this c.1930 tea set are restricted to narrow ribbing on the bodies, and ivory handles (the ivory also has a function as an insulating medium). Wolfers' silver has a pronounced Modernist appearance, often emphasized by geometric motifs. He had a preference for combining different materials in one piece. His silver is always signed; indeed its affinities with the work of Puiforcat and Christofle (see pp. 156-7) are so pronounced that the marks might be regarded as the only distinguishing features.

* Ivory appears frequently on Wolfers' pieces: there was a ready supply from the Belgian Congo in the 20s and 30s.
* Marcel Wolfers should not be confused with his father Philippe, the Art Nouveau jeweller and silversmith.

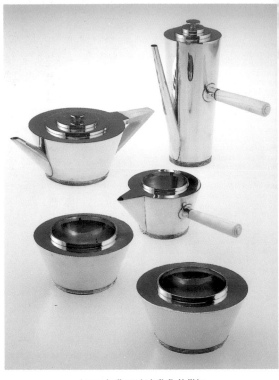

*A tea and coffee service by K. E. M. Weber
c.1930; ht 10in/25.4cm; value code C-D*

Identification checklist for Weber silver and plate
1. Is the piece Modernist in style, with a strong emphasis on form?
2. Does it lack surface decoration or embellishments (except perhaps some reeding or other discreet concession to decoration on any bases or covers)?
3. Are the materials and methods of manufacture innovative?
4. Does the design show a Bauhaus influence (see pp. 142-3)?

Karl Emmanuel Martin (KEM) Weber (American, 1889-1963)
Weber was regarded in the United States as a champion of Modernism. He produced designs for industry, domestic interiors and Hollywood film sets, as well as individually commissioned and mass-produced furniture, ranging from ornately decorative items to comfortably upholstered tubular

metal and sprung steel chairs. His most important work is from after 1927. The tea and coffee service *above*, was designed for the Porter Blanchard company. He also designed for the International Silver Company.

All Weber's designs are sleekly modern yet wholly functional, many showing the influence of the German Bauhaus.

THE INTERNATIONAL SILVER COMPANY
(American 1898-1984)

In 1898 a consortium of more than 30 small manufacturers of silver and plate combined to form one organization, the International Silver Company. Much of the commercial success was generated by the "Hotel Division", which specialized in flatware and holloware for use in hotels, institutions and, during the 1930s, steamships. Most of these wares are of little or no collectable interest, but, during the 1920s and 30s the company employed a number of outside designers, notably Donald Deskey, Weber and Gilbert Rohde, to design useful and decorative wares in silver, plate and pewter.

Many pieces were produced through divisions which used older, prestigious trade marks such as the Wilcox Silver Plate Company; other names include Rogers, and Miller. All pieces bear the mark of the manufacturing company.

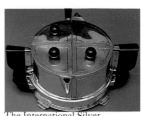

The International Silver Company's late 1920s designs include a series of four-part tea services such as this one, *above*, designed by Gene Theobald. The pot, cream jug and sugar bowl, all in electroplated nickel silver with bakelite handles, are designed to sit snugly in the fitted tray. Pieces such as these are clearly machine-made, although they had to be finished by hand. They are representative of American silver of the time, which was heading away from the European tradition and towards mass-produced industrial design.

* Many items bear the signature of the designer in addition to the company mark.

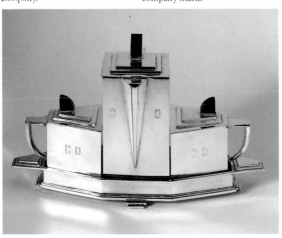

The design for this silver-plated metal tea service with ebony handles, c.1928, was commissioned from the American designer Gilbert Rohde by the International Silver Company, and made under the Wilcox Plate name. (The initials were added by an owner at a later date.) Rohde also designed Modernist chromium cocktail and smoking accessories for the Chase Brass & Copper Company. In the 1930s Chase published an extensive catalogue of its wares, which were mainly inexpensive, chromium-plated items, including smoking paraphernalia, table accessories and some small electrical appliances. Most were of Modernist or whimsical design, and many were innovative. All are marked. Good examples in fine condition are collectable.

Rohde was a highly prolific designer, best known for his furniture produced by the Herman Miller Company and others.

GEORGES FOUQUET

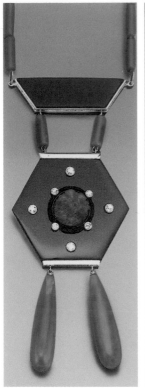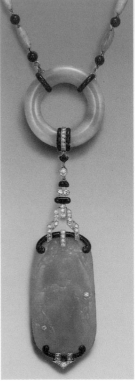

Two pendants designed by Georges Fouquet
both pendants: c.1920; lgth 2¹/₂in/6cm; value code B

Identification checklist for Fouquet jewelry
1. Is the piece symmetrical or does it incorporate symmetrical elements?
2. Does it combine precious and semi-precious materials?
3. If a pendant or a brooch, does it comprise a series of multiple pendants?
4. Are circular and square or rectangular shapes incorporated into one piece?
5. Does the item have an Oriental feel?

Forms and styles
Fouquet's jewelry from the 1920s and 30s is characterized by its use of combined precious and semi-precious materials. In the early 1920s he made mainly high-class pieces in the Parisian tradition, using diamonds and often

exploiting the conflict of black and white. Later he became interested in hardstones, juxtaposed with more transparent precious stones, and he began to use semi-precious stones, such as rock crystal, in significant proportions.

Georges Fouquet (French, 1862-1957)

Fouquet took charge of the high-class Parisian jewellers La Maison Fouquet from his father in 1895. He designed both Art Nouveau and traditional jewelry before taking up the Art Deco style in the 1920s, and continued to work on individual commissions after the house closed in 1936.

Pendants

Fouquet concentrated on making pendants, which are often multiple and use linked sections, as in the pieces in the main picture. Even his brooches have a pendant theme, and some are designed so that they can be worn hung from silk cords. The emphasis is on variety of colour and geometric motifs, which are usually inset, or framed by inset lines of tiny brilliants.

Marks

Pieces are usually signed "Fouquet" or "G. Fouquet".

RAYMOND TEMPLIER (French, 1891-1968)

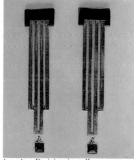

Another Parisian jeweller designing for the luxury market, Raymond Templier made brooches, pins, bangles, pendants and earrings using rigorously geometric forms; these pendant earrings from 1928 suggest Manhattan skyscrapers. Like Fouquet, he was fond of using elongated forms in which circles are combined with verticals. Strong contrasts are achieved by use of matt and polished surfaces. White gold and platinum are also contrasted with pavé set brilliants to give a black and white effect. A number of brooches and pins are in platinum decorated with superimposed enamelled triangles.

JEAN DESPRÈS (French, 1889-1980)

This jeweller's work shows more of a Modernist, almost futuristic, approach than Fouquet's, and makes very little use of gemstones, employing instead semi-precious stones and expensive metals. He concentrated on brooches and solid, chunky rings in abstract geometric patterns influenced by Cubism and African masks. His work is signed "J. Desprès"

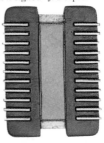

Desprès generally avoided bright colours, preferring greys, blacks and browns. Contrast is achieved through the use of strong relief elements, irregular surfaces and patination, seen in this 1930 brooch

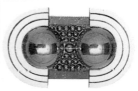

Many of Desprès' jewelry designs recall machine components. This brooch from 1930 is typical, possibly inspired by his period in an aircraft factory during the First World War.

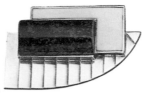

Shapes as well as surfaces and colours were contrasted: lines and curves are juxtaposed in this 1930 brooch, which also shows Desprès' fondness for bloodstone, which he often set against ivory and silver.

165

CARTIER

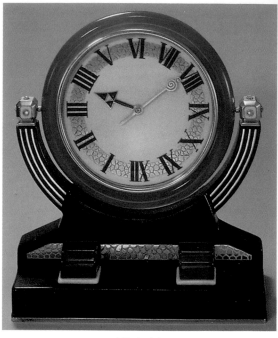

A Cartier clock
c.1930; 6 x 5½in/15.5 x 14cm; value code A

Identification checklist for Cartier clocks
1. Does the clock incorporate superb enamelwork or semi-precious stone inlay?
2. Are any metal mounts either gold or platinum?
3. Does the piece carry a serial number?
4. Is the appearance sculpted?
5. Does the clock show Oriental influences, using chinoiserie?

Cartier (French, 1898-present)
Cartier made a variety of timepieces, but favoured smaller forms such as desk and carriage clocks and the new wristwatches. Traditionally styled pieces continued to be made throughout the 1920s and 30s, but more Modernist pieces were also made.

Clocks were treated almost as sculpture and their elaborate styling means that it is not always immediately apparent what their function is. Designs are often exotic or Oriental. Chinoiserie forms and decorative motifs with a Chinese influence are very common. Semi-precious stones

are often embellished with fine-quality gems.

One of the more popular designs is the roundel mounted on a pediment, seen in this clock, *above*, from 1930, which harks back in form to the Classical shapes of the early 19thC. Although it is relatively sober, it is recognizably "modern", in keeping with the style of the period.
* Materials used were not necessarily expensive: the bakelite of the frame has no intrinsic value, but allows an effect to be achieved which would be impossible with amber, which it resembles.

Collecting

Clocks can be dated by their serial number, which can be checked with Cartier, who keep a record of everything they make.
* Pieces from Cartier in Paris carry more of a premium than those from Cartier in New York or London.

Jewelry

In the Art Deco period Cartier followed the fashion for contemporary shapes, embellishing them with large and colourful gemstones. Pieces were influenced strongly by Oriental, Egyptian and Indian art. Cartier also produced jewelled luxury items, such as powder compacts and cigarette cases.

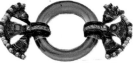

Cartier used jewels to dramatic effect, contrasting red or white against black, as in this rock crystal, ruby and enamel brooch from c.1925. Pieces often make bold use of colour and shape.

VAN CLEEF AND ARPELS (French, 1906 - present)

Together with Cartier and Tiffany, jewelry produced by this firm belongs to the more opulent area of Art Deco design. The firm acquired a reputation for inventive luxury items, including a vanity case known as a *minaudiere* ("simperer"), and a wide range of accessories influenced by Persian, Oriental and medieval art, using coloured gemstones, enamels and lacquer.
* Van Cleef and Arpels pieces can be dated from their serial number.

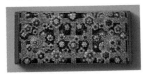

Van Cleef was happy to adopt the new design principles of geometric shapes and contrasting colours, but, as this coral, enamel and diamond powder compact, c.1925 shows, used plain designs and shapes as a foil for a profusion of gemstones rather than enamels and semi-precious stones.

TIFFANY & CO. (United States, 1837-present)

In the United States, Tiffany created pieces for an elitist market, but the conservative tastes of rich America meant that there was very little demand for high-fashion jewelry. The new stylistic trends are more evident in the company's clocks. These often show a Chinese influence and make much use of precious stones, especially diamonds.

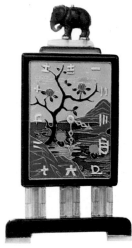

This small Tiffany clock, only 5in (12.7cm) high, is a mixture of relatively plain, modernistic cabinet and support and the traditional luxury of Tiffany items. There is a typical combination of jewelled opulence, Modernistic form and pseudo-Oriental embellishments: there is a green jade elephant, and pseudo-Chinese characters are used as numerals. However, the treatment of the landscape is very European, especially the clouds. The bold colours are characteristic.
* Tiffany pieces were made primarily for the American market, although examples can be found elsewhere. They are usually signed.
* The work of Tiffany & Co., the jewellers, should not be confused with that of Tiffany Studios, run by Louis Comfort Tiffany. The Studios did make some geometric lampshades in the 1920s and 30s, which often prove less popular than their earlier creations.

167

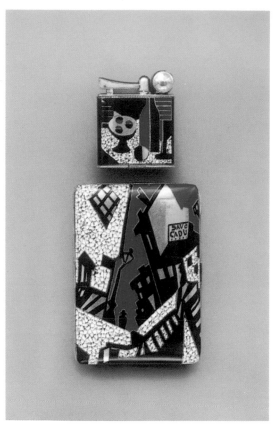

A matching lighter and cigarette case by Gerard Sandoz
c.1925; ht 3¹/₂in/8.5cm; value code C

Identification checklist for the jewelry and accessories designed by Gerard Sandoz

1. Does the decoration contain geometric or Cubistic elements?
2. Is the piece signed?
3. Is the form clean and simple?
4. Is there a contrast of primary colours?
5. Does the design suggest a machine influence, particularly in its use of contrasting metals and surface finishes for decorative impact?
6. Is the piece hand-made?
7. If jewelry, is there a combination of semi- or non-precious materials and stones?
8. Does the piece combine a number of different materials – for example, eggshell, silver and lacquer?

Gerard Sandoz (French, b.1902)

Sandoz, who trained with his father Gustave Roger-Sandoz, is among the most inventive craftsmen of the period, and one of the most commercial. He hand-made small, individual luxury items, such as fine quality lighters, boxes and cigarette cases, as well as pendants and brooches, which belong almost exclusively to the 1920s. Unusually for work made for a luxury market, very little emphasis is placed on precious stones, although precious metals, such as gold, sometimes appear. Sandoz is particularly noted for his use of eggshell, lacquer and niello work, and for his juxtaposition of materials and surfaces to give a textured effect.

Marks

Pieces are usually marked and may bear the signature of both father and son. The niello and silver cigarette case shown below is signed "GERARD SANDOZ"; the lighter and cigarette case shown left are signed "Gerard Sandoz and G. Roger Sandoz".

Niello work

This term is used for silver and black lacquerwork, made by letting in thin lacquer onto a silver surface, which is then polished. Niello work was popularized in Russia in the 19thC and was favoured in Europe during the 1920s and 30s.

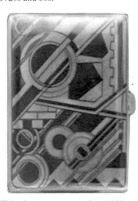

This cigarette case, made c.1925, is typical of Sandoz in its use of niello and its highly geometric pattern of industrial gears and other motifs suggestive of modern machine components.

JEAN GOULDEN (French, 1878-1947)

Primarily an enameller, Jean Goulden produced table lamps, clocks and other decorative items. Some of his designs were executed by Jean Dunand (see pp. 18-19), from whom Goulden learned the craft of enamelling.

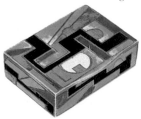

Most of Goulden's enamel designs were executed on silver, as with this 1927 cigarette box, or other precious metals, using the champlevé technique in which the silver is cut into and the enamels laid in the cloissons, or reservoirs. Although the use of enamel was quite common during this period, Goulden was unusual in introducing texture through the use of degraded or irregular surfaces; the resulting grained effect is evident in this box. Another characteristic of Goulden's enamel work is that he uses areas of the base metal, in this case silver, as part of the decoration. Geometric patterns invariably dominate. Most items are signed.

PAUL-EMILE BRANDT (Swiss, dates unknown)

Paul Brandt made small luxury items such as boxes, cigarette cases and jewelry, especially bracelets, clips and bracelet-watches. The items that turn up for sale most frequently are those that contain an element of lacquerwork. His designs of the 1920s and 30s are strongly geometric, using materials such as gold and platinum combined with precious stones to create a luxurious item. Although similar to Sandoz's work, Brandt's pieces are often identifiable, not only by their use of precious stones but by:
* the use of more clearly defined opposing areas of colour
* a strong symmetrical element
* a chevron motif
* the use of black enamel or black onyx.

MINOR SILVER AND JEWELRY

Although exclusive pieces use expensive jewels and materials and are signed by major artists, there are a number of other items available which, despite their use of less expensive materials and lack of a well-known signature, are nicely made and evocative of the time, and are therefore worth collecting.

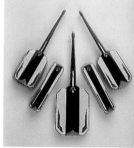

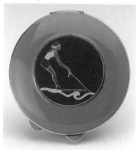

The powder compact was developed to its full potential during the 1920s and 30s. Handbags, which were considered an essential accessory, were narrow, so any accoutrements had to be slim and delicate. This characteristic example is enamel on silver and depicts an independent sporty 30s woman. However, the work is not of the highest quality and the piece is unmarked.

The English made a variety of designs for dressing table sets, a medium which found fresh inspiration in the period. This brush set is decorated with fan motifs in diamanté and guilloche enamel, and the silver mounts have English hallmarks.
* Sets of this kind are desirable. However, the brushes tend to need replacing relatively often and this is an expensive exercise which deters some buyers.
* Sets should be complete, as here, and are worth even more if other fittings are also included, such as a hair tidy, ring tree, candlesticks, powder box and cover, talc tube and cover or matching jewelry box.
Sometimes, especially if they are German, all these come in a fitted tray.

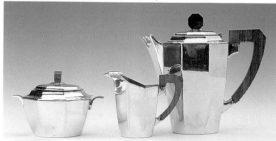

A number of cube teapots were produced in silver and plate, especially in Birmingham and Sheffield. This English silver service with pseudo-panel form, although inspired by French designs, falls short of pieces by top designers as the forms are too heavily compromised by early 19thC shapes. It is not by any known maker. There are a number of minor services of this type available: these sold well at the time they were made, as they were affordable to the general public. The minimum set comprises coffee pot, milk jug and sugar bowl. Sunray motifs were sometimes the only decoration that might be applied.
* Coffee sets were relatively new to the period, becoming popular as coffee acquired a more fashionable status, and usually incorporated silver spoons with coffee bean terminals.

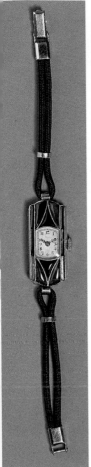

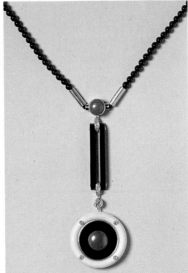

Avant-garde jewelry by top French designers was emulated by other French makers. This pendant is well made and uses similar materials to those on good pieces – ivory and brilliant diamonds – and the only reason it is considered minor is that it cannot be definitely attributed. However, as a fine quality item it may prove a better investment than an expensive signed piece, especially as new attributions are coming to light all the time.

This watch, with its black shoelace strap, is typical of the form and design popular in the 1920s and 30s, but suffers from the absence of diamonds, marcasite or even paste stones. The only decoration the watch has is made of glass cabochons simulating sapphires. The maker is unknown.
* Watches should be in working order. The strap need not be original.

This rectangular compact in lacquered tinplate is probably French as it employs a clever photoprinting technique to simulate crushed eggshell, which was very much a French forte. The piece is extremely lightweight and even flimsy, but does fit the purpose for which

it was intended, and at first glance appears to be made of expensive materials. The handles at the top allow it to be hung on a chain. Although there is no maker's mark, the strong period feel makes it collectable nevertheless.
* Small, unattributed cigarette cases offer another fruitful area for those who wish to make up a relatively inexpensive collection of jewelry and accessories.

171

RUGS

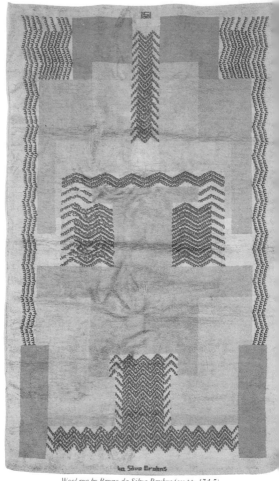

Wool rug by Bruno da Silva Bruhus (see pp. 174-5)

Until the end of the 19thC, many of the rugs found in Britain
emanated from the Middle East or from the French
Savonnerie works. However, in the early 20thC the rug
enjoyed something of a revival, promoted by, amongst others,
the firm of William Morris & Co. in London, which paved the
way for an increased interest in British and European textiles
generally, although the number of designers making rugs in
the modern style remained small compared with craftsmen
producing modern designs in other media. The role of the rug
was re-evaluated (as had happened temporarily under
Morris): it was no longer merely a decorative floor cover
unrelated to the decor and furnishings of the room, but was

elevated to the status of a work of art. Decorative effect took precedence over considerations of utility and practicality.

In Britain, the best rugs were commissioned. The firms of Axminster, Wilton Royal, Edinburgh Weavers and Templeton commissioned work from a number of major designers, among them Eileen Gray, Frank Brangwyn, Marion Dorn and Edward MacKnight Kauffer.

During the 1920s and 30s many rugs were also imported into Britain from Belgium. These often have abstract patterns or motifs and are usually in sombre colours. They tend to be symmetrical, made in two parts joined by a central seam. Most are by anonymous designers.

In France as elsewhere, the best rugs of the period were commissioned, many for Exhibitions or luxury liners. Paris ensembliers included rugs in their lavish ranges of interior furniture, many were made by the top designers of the day such as Jacques-Emile Ruhlmann, Paul Follot, Jean Lurcat, Jules Leleu and the firm of Süe et Mare.

In the United States, Ruth Reeves designed some rugs for W. & J. Sloane that evoked American city life, such as *Manhattan*, as well as a series dominated by Cubist and geometric motifs. Top designers in other media also turned their attention to textiles – for example, Donald Deskey, Gilbert Rohde, Eugene Schoen and Loja Saarinen – who designed some rugs for the influential Cranbrook Academy.

Rugs were varied in shape, and no longer restricted to simple rectangles; some are round. Colours were no longer dark and sombre as they had been (presumably largely for practical reasons). Many rugs from the 1920s and 30s are very pale, and tend toward autumnal and subdued tones of brown, green, black, grey, or delicate pastels. McKnight Kauffer's rugs, executed in bold primary colours, are exceptions. Designers also dispensed with fringing and borders, and with the symmetry that had dominated earlier designs. Inspiration for motifs now came from Africa or Cubism; or were Mayan and Aztec. Geometric designs lent themselves particularly well to the large flat, palette-like expanse of a rug. However, not all rugs of the 1920s and 30s contained geometric or abstract motifs. French rugs in particular continued to incorporate stylized floral motifs in *"millefiori"* (thousand flower) designs, and many of them display the influence of foremost artists, such as Paul Cezanne and Raoul Dufy, whose distinctive palettes complemented the furnishings of "modern" interiors.

Rugs of the period tend to be well-made and solid, with canvas backing, intended for use on floors rather than as wall hangings. The pile is regular, as they are usually machine-woven (although a few were hand-woven), and the most common material is wool. They are often signed by the designer, which is rare in any other period. The wool is subject to fading, so strong colours are often at a premium. Examine the back to determine the density of the knots – the more knots per square inch the better.

BRUNO DA SILVA BRUHNS

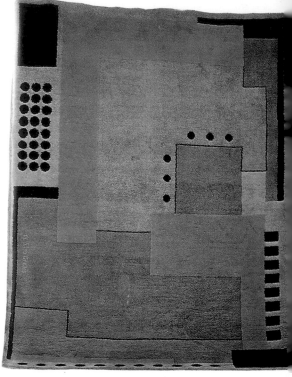

*A rug designed by Da Silva Bruhns
c.1928; 152 x 114in/386 x 289.5cm; value code B*

Identification checklist for Da Silva Bruhns rugs
1. Is the rug signed?
2. Are the colours harmonious, perhaps in coordinating muted tones?
3. If the design is asymmetrical, does it consist of geometric motifs around, or enclosed within, rectangular or square-shaped panels outlined in black?
4. Do circles or polka dots feature in asymmetrical designs?
5. If the design is symmetrical does it exhibit Aztec/Mayan influences?
6. Is the rug made of hand-knotted wool?

Signatures and Authenticity
Bruhns used his full signature and/or monogram. The rug shown *above*, fairly typically, has both – the signature along the side and the initials across the top. A carpet signed by da Bruhns is almost certainly genuine, as fakes are not known to have been produced. The design sketches he made for 174

his rugs and carpets are also collectable. These are usually framed and may also bear his signature. More of his work is available in New York and Paris than in England. Unlike McKnight-Kauffer, who was a commercial designer for Axminster, Bruhns did mostly commissioned work.

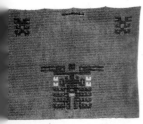

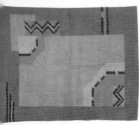

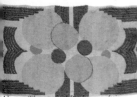

Above: *Three typical Bruhns rug designs from the early 1930s.*

BETTY JOEL (Anglo-Chinese, 1896-1984)

A contemporary of Bruhns, Betty Joel was born in China and went to live in England in 1919, where she opened a furniture and textile shop. She later moved to Surrey and took showrooms in Knightsbridge, London. During the 1920s her work trod a fine line between the traditional and the avant-garde, becoming more geometric and simpler in the 30s. She was not a prolific rug maker; most pieces were commissioned, and thus of high quality and very expensive.

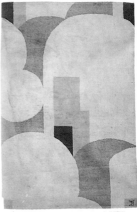

This rug from c.1930-5, shows Joel's preference for circles and stepped effects. (These also appear as part of the structure or decoration of her furniture, see pp. 32-3.) Designs were often assymmetrical, as here. The palette is subtle and harmonious; colours are not outlined, but simply laid one over the other, their density giving a depth of field. The rugs were made in China and signed with a distinctive Chinese-looking monogram, which resembles a Ming character mark (visible in the bottom right-hand corner of this rug).

Bruno da Silva Bruhns (French, dates unknown)

Bruhns worked in Paris, where many of his pieces were manufactured by the Savonnerie works. He contributed to many major exhibitions. His designs are characterized by a preference for geometric motifs and layouts, and for circles or polka dot motifs. They usually have a degree of intricacy. Piano key and comb effects also appear quite frequently in his work. Motifs are occasionally given a thin outline. Bruhns was influenced by a number of different cultures and idioms: he was adapting Colonial motifs as early as the 1920s, and in the mid-20s and 30s he added to his decorative repertoire American-Indian and North African and Cubistic elements. Colours are subtle and muted rather than violent, and though they may contrast with each other, never clash but are well-blended. Quality is always high in Bruhns carpets.

The Myrbor Studio

Among other influential and now collectable rugs of the Art Deco period are those made in the Myrbor Studio in Northern Africa in the ten years or so from 1925. The designs were the work of several artists, such as Jean Lurcat, Fernand Léger, Joan Miró and Jean Arp.

175

EDWARD McKNIGHT KAUFFER

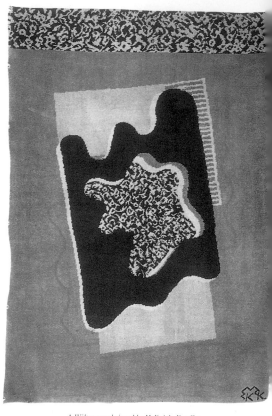

A Wilton rug designed by McKnight Kauffer
Early 1930s; 90 x 59¹/₂in/229 x 151cm; value code C

Identification checklist for Kauffer rugs and carpets
1. Is bold use made of colours?
2. Is the design strongly asymmetrical?
3. Is the piece signed with a monogram in the bottom right-hand corner?
4. Is the rug without border, fringe or tassels?
5. Is the pile very deep?

Edward McKnight Kauffer (Britain, 1890-1954)
Kauffer was American-born, but spent the major part of his working life in Britain. He collaborated with his wife, Marion Dorn, on commercial rug designs for the British firm Wilton Royal Carpets as well as working to commission for a very select
176

market. Many rugs were designed to act as an integral part of a room setting, and were intended to complement other aspects of the interior design.

Rugs by Kauffer do not tend to use the fringed edging or patterned border traditional on rugs before 1920. They are well-made, with a deep pile.

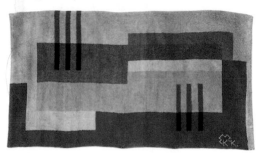

Style

Kauffer's rugs show a strong preference for vivid, often unusual, shades and combinations: the rug in the main picture, which incorporates angular and curvilinear elements, is a typical but relatively subdued example of his work, showing Cubist elements. Stripes and blocks of colour sometimes overlap, and frequent use is made of a comb effect, as on the two examples here. The interplay of shape and form gives the rugs a strong three-dimensional quality, sometimes reinforced by an animal-skin motif.

Kauffer's work is strongly Modernist. This example, *above*, in beige, brown, salmon pink and grey, is typical in its use of an asymmetrical geometric design of rectangular motifs with red and black bands. It makes use of the interplay between horizontals and verticals, with the comb effect again visible; curved elements are absent. Typically, Kauffer's monogram can be clearly seen in the bottom right-hand corner.
* Kauffer was also a poster designer: his best-known designs are for London Transport and Shell Petroleum.

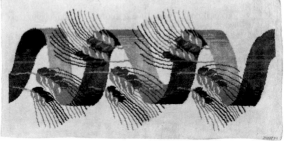

MARION DORN (British, 1900-64)

Kauffer's wife Dorn was a very different type of designer from her husband. Her rugs show greater sensitivity to the textile medium, using more organic colours, rather than imposing the ideas of formal art movements. She was known as the "architect of floors", and her rugs were sold through the London department store Fortnum and Mason. Some were made as commissions for large London hotels. In 1934 she established her own firm, Marion Dorn Ltd, specializing in custom-designed and handmade rugs. She made more rugs than Kauffer. Dorn's designs are less strongly

rectilinear than those by Kauffer, and often feature interlaced circles, loop patterns, sometimes symmetrical and sometimes free-flowing, and waves. Knot and puzzle effects are also common. This example, *above*, is typical of Dorn's work, incorporating organic imagery with a sweeping curved line. Her colours are subtle and subdued, tending towards autumnal tones, especially shades of brown and grey. On some pieces the pile is cut to give a textural, layered effect. Her rugs are usually signed "DORN" in block letters. Both Kauffer's and Dorn's rugs should also carry the factory label.

MINOR RUGS

Rugs from the 1920s and 30s turn up fairly frequently at auction and many are surprisingly affordable. The most prized examples are those with Modernist or other avant-garde designs, and bright colours. Many less expensive examples are so because they are unsigned, or because they show excessive signs of wear. Some rug designers of the period attempted to emulate the most successful designs of the period but occasionally misinterpreted them – for example, by choosing colours that are too dull, or by crowding the piece with over-elaborate patterns.

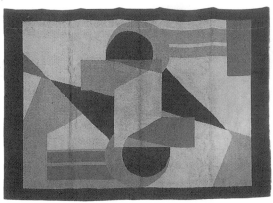

This rug, with its bold geometric design in tones of brown and its juxtaposition of circles and triangles, is decidedly Modernist, and the piece is in good condition, although a little faded. Because it is unsigned it is likely to be inexpensive and therefore good value.
* The bright colours of the 1920s gave way in the 1930s to more subdued tones and greater interest in texture.

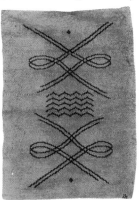

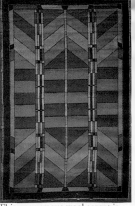

This pleasingly simple Ian Henderson rug, *above*, from c.1930 is hand-woven, and uses a design reminiscent of the work of Marion Dorn (see p. 177) and typical of the Art Deco period generally. It is also monogrammed in the corner, although the designer is not well-known.

This anonymous wool carpet is decorated with bold geometric motifs in the typical period colours of iron red, yellow and brown. The zigzag design is a recurring theme of the Art Deco years and was used very successfully in a variety of media, but here the pattern is rather fussy.

178

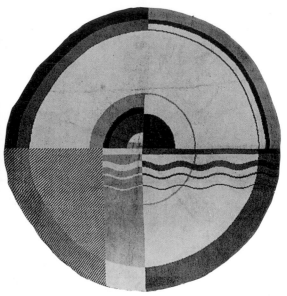

This circular tufted rug, also from the 1930s, is divided into quarters, each with a geometric arc or linear motif in deep red, blue or black on a beige background. The unusual shape and strong design make such a rug desirable despite being unsigned and such a piece is likely to prove a good investment.

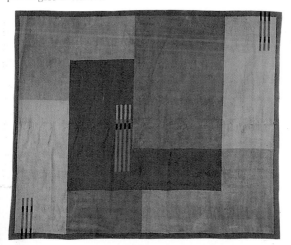

This Axminster rug is part of the Romney seamless range produced by Templeton's in the 1930s. The designer is not known. These rugs were unusual in that they were made in one piece, unlike most large rugs of the time. The bands of black and orange are similar to the comb motif used by MacKnight Kauffer (see p. 176), but the remainder is in sober grey/green colours. The design can be traced to a small catalogue produced by Templeton's in the 1930s.

GLOSSARY

Acid-cutting Method of decorating glass by which the objects are coated with wax or another acid-resistant substance, then incised with a fine steel point and dipped in acid.

Amboyna Mottled, highly grained wood of an Indonesian tree.

Aquatint Method of etching whereby acidic resin is applied to a copper plate and heated so that areas acquire a pitted surface which then transfers ink to paper.

Arts and Crafts Late 19thC movement advocating simple, solid, hand-made construction, using the natural beauty of materials to artistic effect.

Bakelite Synthetic resin, or plastic. Usually in dark colours.

Bauhaus style In the style of the German Bauhaus movement – that is, designed according to demands of machine production, relating construction to function.

Car mascot Ornamental badge or device to be mounted on a car radiator cap.

Chryselephantine An expensive combination of ivory and a metal, usually bronze.

Cire perdue The French term for "lost wax", a process that results in unique casts.

Crackled glaze (*craquelure*) Deliberate cracked effect achieved by firing ceramics to a precise temperature.

Cubism Formal art movement characterized by distortion, angularity, geometric arrangements and features of African sculpture.

Dinanderie Work in non-precious metals.

Electroplate Silver-plated ware produced by electrolyzing silver on to base metal.

Etching Type of engraving in which the design, drawn with an etching needle on a copper plate coated with an acid-resistant, is dipped in acid, then used to transfer ink to paper.

Gesso Ground made from plaster mixed with size, used to prepare a panel or canvas for gilding.

Gouache Opaque water colour painting. Pigments are bound with glue.

Ivorene Worthless plastic substance resembling ivory.

Limed oak Oak coated with lime which is then brushed off to leave a white residue in the grain.

Lithograph Print made from stone on which a design is drawn in ink and fixed. The remaining porous areas are treated with water so that the printing ink adheres only to the design, which is then transferred to the paper.

Macassar A rare form of ebony.

Marquetry Furniture decoration in which shapes are cut into a sheet of wood veneer and inlaid with other woods or materials.

Martelé Metal formed into shapes by hammering.

Modernism/Functionalism International movement in 1930s furniture design. Clean lines and the cube shape were emphasized.

Opalescent Translucent white glass; a reddish core is visible when held up to the light.

Pâte de cristal Almost transparent glass made of powdered glass paste which has fused in a mould.

Pâte de verre Translucent glass similar to pâte de cristal but with a lower proportion of lead.

Patination Alteration to the surface appearance of metal caused by time, use or chemical corrosion.

Pavé setting Stones set so close together that no backing material is visible.

Plywood Form of laminated wood with the grain of alternate layers set at right angles.

Pochoir Reproduction process using different stencils for each colour of a print, applied over a black and white reproduction of the original.

Raku Form of Japanese earthenware covered with a thick lead glaze.

Sgraffito Carved-away decoration on pottery.

Slipware Earthenware decorated with designs trailed in or incised through a mixture of clay (slip).

Streamlining Style with flowing curved lines and aerodynamic form, prevalent in 1930s American design.

Transfer-printing Method by which a design is printed in ink on an engraved copper plate and transferred to paper, which is then pressed on the ceramic surface while still wet.

Woodcut Print made by drawing the design on the surface of a block of wood and cutting away the parts to remain white in the picture. The surface is then inked and transferred to paper.

Ziggurat Stepped pyramid-shaped pedestal of marble or onyx for small bronze figures.

SELECTED DESIGNERS
MANUFACTURERS & RETAILERS

Aalto, Alvar (1898-1976)
Finnish Modernist architect and
furniture designer. Director of
Finmar and founder of Artek
(1931), both furnishing
companies.

Argy-Rousseau, Gabriel (1885-1953)
French designer of pâte de verre
and pâte de cristal glass objects.

Baccarat (estabd 1764)
French glass company; best
known for paperweights, and
enamelled and geometric wares.

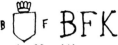

Bauhaus (1919-1933)
German design school. Founded
by the architect **Walter
Gropius**, it included architects,
engineers, designers, sculptors
and painters, who sought to relate
form to function and aesthetic
qualities to the demands of
machine production. Pure
geometrical forms are at the heart
of much Bauhaus design.

Franz Bergman (dates unknown)
Viennese sculptor, best known for
his erotic bronzes of women.
Mark: "Namgreb" (anagram of
name).

Boch Frères (estabd 1841)
Belgian ceramics firm; a branch of
the German company Villeroy &
Boch. Produced brightly
decorated crackled white wares.

**Bouraine, Marcel (dates
unknown)**
French sculptor, best known for
his Amazon figures in silvered and
patinated bronze. Mark: "M.A.
Bouraine".

Brandt, Edgar-William (1880-1960)
French designer and metalworker,
best known for his fine wrought
iron work, sometimes burnished
or painted a silver colour.

E BRANDT

Breuer, Marcel 1902-81
Hungarian-born architect and
furniture designer; studied
interior design at the Bauhaus.

Used wood and tubular steel in
his designs. Moved from England
to the United States in 1937.
Unmarked, although his designs
for Thonet and DIM have
makers' labels and PEL and
Standard-Mobel catalogues note
some of his steel chairs.

Buthaud, Rene (1886-1986)
French painter and artist potter,
best known for African-inspired
decoration. Marks: "R. Buthaud"
painted; "RB", incised or painted.

Cardew, Michael (1901-1983)
English artist potter working in
earthernware slip, pupil of
Bernard Leach. Worked from
Winchcombe Pottery in
Gloucestershire, 1926-39.
Experimented with tin glazes on
his large vessels.

Carlton ware (estabd 1897)
Brand name used by Wiltshaw &
Robinson, a pottery founded in
1897 in Stoke-on-Trent. Marks:
"W&R/STOKE ON TRENT"
forming a circle which encloses a
swallow, topped by a crown;
"Carlton ware" hand painted over
name and address of firm.

Cartier (estabd 1898)
Jewelers founded in Paris in 1898.
Opened in London (1903) and
New York (1912).

Cartier

**Cassandre, Adolphe-Jean-Marie
Mouron, (1901-68)**
French artist and leading posterist
in a geometrical manner.

A.M. CASSANDRE

**Chiparus, Dimitri (Dèmetre)
(dates unknown)**
Rumanian-born sculptor who
worked in Paris in the 1920s.

Christofle, Orfevrerie
Metalwork manufacturers,
founded 1829 in Paris.

Cliff, Clarice (1899-1972)
English potter, designer and
decorator. Art director at
Wilkinson's Royal Staffordshire
Pottery and its subsidiary,
Newport Pottery. Cliff also
decorated wares designed by

MAKERS

other artists. Mark: black printed pottery mark, name of design and facsmilie signature.

Colin, Paul (born 1892)
French designer and posterist, most renowned designs being for *Les Ballets Suédois and Le Ballet Nègre*. Mark: printed signature "PAUL COLIN".

Colinet, Jeanne Robert (dates unknown)
French sculptor; Mark: "J.R. Colinet".

Compagnie des Arts Francais
See **Süe et Mare.**

Cooper, Susie (born 1902)
English potter. Designed for A. E. Gray & Co. (c.1925), especially bright geometrical forms. Formed her own company in 1932.

Daum Frères (estabd 1875)
French glassworks established by brothers Auguste (1853-1909) and Antonin (1864-1930) Daum, working principally in pâte de verre.

Decoeur, Émile (1876-1953)
French artist potter.

Décorchement, Françoise-Emile (1880-1971)
French glass maker, exponent of pâte de verre and pâte de cristal.

Deskey, Donald (1894-1989)
American architect and designer, using geometric motifs. Mark: "Deskey-Vollmer".

De Stijl (estabd 1917)
Influential Dutch association of artists, 1917-31, favouring primary colours and abstract, rectangular forms, and rejecting ornament.

Deutscher Werkbund (estabd 1907)
Association of artists, architects, manufacturers and writers formed in Munich.

Marion Dorn (1899-1964)
American-born textile designer, living in London. Rug designs

made by Wilton Royal Carpet Factory.

DORN

Doulton Lambeth potteries (estabd 1815)
The Art department of Doulton & Co. English pottery manufacturers founded by Henry Doulton and John Sparkes, head of the Lambeth School of Art.

Dryden, Ernst (dates unknown)
Leading Austrian graphic designer. Marks: "Deutsch"; "Dryden".

Dufrêne, Maurice (1876-1955)
French designer of furniture, ceramics, metal, glass and carpets. Later work included Modernist designs using tubular steel.

Dupas, Jean (1882-1964)
French painter, muralist and poster artist. Mark: dated and signed "Jean Dupas" at the bottom.

Etling (active 1920s, 30s)
Paris firm which commissioned and distributed work by many designers.

Finmar (estabd 1934/5)
Finnish furniture manufacturers headed by **Alvar Aalto,** producing items in laminated wood. Unmarked, although the *Decorative Arts Journal* shows the full range of their wares, and pieces made by Aalto in Finland are marked "Aalto Möbler, Svensk Kvalitet Sprodurt".

Follot, Paul (1877-1941)
French interior decorator and designer, an early exponent of Art Deco. Unmarked, but some have characteristic "Follot rose".

Fouquet, Georges (1862-1957)
French goldsmith and jeweller. Joined his father's Paris firm in 1891 and took over in 1895, on his father's retirement.

G. FOUQUET

Frankl, Paul (1886-1958)
Austrian architect and furniture designer; settled in the United States in 1914. Used Californian redwood, and silver leaf in his predominantly city-style designs. Mark: metal tag with name of manufacturer.

Gesmar, Charles (1900-28)
French artist and posterist;
designed posters for the *Folies-Bergère*.

Goldscheider, Marcel (1885-1953)
Austrian ceramics manufacturer,
founded factory in 1886 making
Art Nouveau vases and later Art
Deco figures.

Goupy, Marcel (1886-1954 retd)
French artist and glass and
pottery designer. Mark: signature.
Gropius, Walter (1883-1969)
German architect, founder of the
Bauhaus and director until 1928.
Exponent of Modernist
principles. His multi-combination
modular furniture (1927) was
highly influential.
Groult, André (1884-1967)
French interior decorator and
furniture designer who used
luxurious embellishments (velvet,
ivory, and shark skin) in his
rythmic furniture designs.
Hagenauer (estabd 1898)
Austrian foundry based in Vienna,
known for its face masks and
figures inspired by Negro art.

Heal, Sir Ambrose (1872-1959)
English cabinet-maker and
director of family firm, Heal &
Son. He used many woods in his
designs and, eventually, steel and
aliminium. Mark: stamped or
labelled company name.
Heals, Gordon Russell (1892-1980)
English furniture designer who
specialized in pale veneers.
Hunebelle, André (active 1920s)
French glass artist inspired by
Lalique. Mark: "A. Hunebelle",
impressed.
Isokon Furniture Co.(estabd 1931)
English furniture manufacturers,
established by Jack Pritchard.
Made mass-produced items in the
modern style.
Jensen, Georg (1866 -1935)
Primarily a silversmith

specializing in high-quality
silverware and jewelry. Mark:
stamped.

Joel, Betty (1896-1984)
English furniture and rug
designer. Produced functional
pieces for the smaller home.
Company marks: on furniture,
signatures of designer and
craftsman with date on card under
glass; on rugs, woven monogram.

La Faguays, Pierre (dates unknown)
French sculptor.
Lalique, René (1860-1945)
French glassmaker, famous for his
scent bottles. The Lalique works
also produced glass screens,
lamps, innovative car mascots,
fountains and lights. Marks: "R.
Lalique, France" in script with
model number; same number
engraved on stopper and base of
bottle.

R LALIQUE

Leach, Bernard (1887-1979)
English architect potter.
Decoration included stamped,
stencilled, inlaid, modelled and
slip work. Made raku earthenware
using a Japanese technique of
hand-modelling.

Le Corbusier, Charles Edouard Jeanneret (1887-1965)
Swiss Modernist architect and
designer; became French citizen
in 1930. Designed machine-made
goods for mass market, using
tubular steel with leather and
hides.
Lenoble, Emile (1876-1939)
French artist potter influenced by
Oriental ceramics.
Limoges
French ceramics centre with
significant output of mass-produced Art Deco porcelain.

Lorenzl, Josef (dates unknown)
Austrian sculptor.

Luce, Jean (1895-1964)
French designer. Sold porcelain and faience tableware from his Paris store, 1920s. Mark: Painted crossed "LL" in rectangle.

Marinot, Maurice 1882-1960
French painter, sculptor and glass designer; produced mostly vases.

McKnight-Kauffer, Edward (1890-1954)
American artist and posterist working in Britain; designed posters for London Underground.

Meissen (estabd early 18thC)
German pottery manufacturers, established early 18thC. Commissioned tableware and figures. Mark: variations of crossed swords mark; 1924-34 dot between sword blades.

Mies van der Rohe, Ludwig (1886-1969)
German Modernist architect and an innovative and influential furniture designer. Vice-president of Deutscher Werkbund, 1926; 1930-33 director of the Bauhaus; 1937 moved to America. Pieces unmarked.

Miklos, Gustave (1888-1967)
Hungarian sculptor, best known for his all-bronze primitive figures made in limited editions.

Murray, Keith (1893-1981)
New Zealand-born architect and designer, settled in England 1935. Designed silver and pottery and, from 1932, glass. Marks: "Keith Murray" over fleur de lys.

Nash, Paul (1889-1946)
English painter and illustrator. A war artist in both World Wars, he was a central figure in the British avant-garde movement and formed Unit One in 1933 to popularize Modernist thinking.

Navarre, Henri (1885-1970)
French glass artist. His sculptural, textured vases and bowls were influenced by Marinot. Mark: "Henri Navarre".

Orrefors (estabd 1898)
Swedish glassworks. From 1915 produced decorative glassware designed by Edvard Hald and Simon Gate, amongst others.

Poertzel, Otto (born 1876)
German sculptor. Mark: "Prof. Poertzel".

Poole Pottery
Originally Carter, Stabler & Adams. Partnership formed 1921 at Poole, Dorset. Traded as Poole Pottery Ltd from 1963.

Practical Equipment Limited
English manufacturers of tubular steel frame chairs and steel and glass furnishings.

Preiss, Ferdinand (1882-1943)
German sculptor. Opened foundry in 1906. Mark: "F Preiss"; foundry mark "PK".

Primavera
Pottery department of the Au Printemps store in Paris. Outlet for the work of various artists.

Pritchard, Jack (born 1899)
English manufacturer of laminated wood furniture, distributed through his Isokon retail outlet.

Rateau, Armand-Albert (1882-1938)
French interior decorator and furniture designer. Work epitomized by fine decoration in patinated bronze, lacquerwork, marble and ivory.

Rietveld, Gerrit Thomas (1888-1964)
Dutch architect and furniture designer. Joined De Stijl, the Dutch artists' association, in 1919; the geometric forms, primary colours and revealed construction of his furniture epitomize the work of the group.

Rivière, Guiraud (dates unknown)
French sculptor and metalworker. Mark: "GUIRAUD-RIVIERE".

Rosenthal (estabd 1879)
Bavarian porcelain factory. Marks: crossed lines with artist's mark and sometimes "RC"; crown over all marks.

Royal Copenhagen (estabd 1773)
Danish pottery factory which made Chinese-style porcelain with crystalline glazes and stoneware. Marks: crown and three waves motif with "Danmark" or "Royal Copenhagen".

Ruhlmann, Emile-Jacques (1879-1933)
French painter, master-cabinet-maker from 1925. Mark: branded signature.

Sabino, Marius Ernest (active 1920s and 30s)
French glass architect inspired by Lalique. Mark: "Sabino, France"

Paul Scheurich born 1883
Porcelain modeller, born in New York; worked in Germany.

Sèvres (estabd 1756)
French porcelain factory.

Shelley potteries
The name from 1925 of Foley, pottery firm established 1860 in Staffordshire, England.

Phoebe Stabler (died 1955)
English sculptor and designer. Made ceramic figures, enamels and jewelry with her husband Harold. Mark: "STABLER, HAMMERSMITH, LONDON" with date and mould number.

Staite Murray, William (1881-1962)
English engineer, painter and potter. Influenced by Japanese artist-potter, Shoji Hamada, he made stoneware with scratched or brushed decoration and partial glazing.

Steuben Glass Works (estabd 1903)
American glass manufacturers.

Süe, Louis (1875-1968) and Mare, André (1887-1932)
French furniture, carpet and textile designers who collaborated on ornate furniture in the French high Deco style. Unmarked.

Teague, Walter Dorwin (1883-1960)
American industrial designer.

Work includes Modernist art glass for **Steuben**.

Thonet Brothers (Gebrüder Thonet, Thonet Frères)
Furniture manufacturers established in Vienna, 1853. Designed and manufactured bentwood furniture, largely for export. Designers included Le Corbusier and Mies van der Rohe. Marks: variations on name, stamped or on label.

Thuret, André (1898-1965)
French glass artist. His sculptural designs were inventive.

Walter, Alméric (1859-1942)
French glass artist, known for his pate de verre glass.

Waugh, Sidney B. (1904-63)
American sculptor and glass designer. Designer for Steuben Glass Works, 1933. Marks: engraved series numbers on limited edition pieces.

Wedgwood (estabd 1759)
English pottery company. Marks: "WEDGWOOD, Made in England"

Wiener Werkstätte (Viennese Workshops) (estabd 1903)
Association of artist-craftsmen who sought to combine utility and aesthetic qualities in furniture, metalwork and building designs.

A. J. Wilkinson Ltd (estabd 1896)
English pottery company. Factories included Royal Staffordshire Pottery and Newport Pottery. Clarice Cliff was art director, although the company also produced the designs of other artists – for example, Vanessa Bell and Duncan Grant.

Wright, Frank Lloyd (1867-1959)
American architect and designer, father of the Prairie School of architecture. His Modernist principles – the use of pure forms, modern materials and modern techniques of construction – concurred with much Art Deco thinking. Pieces are unsigned although usually well-documented.

Zach, Bruno (dates unknown)
Austrian sculptor, best known for his erotic figures. Mark: "Zach".

BIBLIOGRAPHY

Arwas, Victor, *Art Deco*, 1980
Art Deco Sculpture, 1975
Glass – Art Nouveau to Art Deco, 1977
Batkin, Maureen, *Wedgwood Ceramics 1846-1959*, 1982
Battersby, Martin, *The Decorative Twenties*, 1969
The Decorative Twenties, 1971
Bauhaus, Exhibition Catalogue, Royal Academy, 1973
Bayer, Patricia and Waller, Mark, *The Art of René Lalique*, 1988
British Art and Design 1900-1960 Exhibition Catalogue, V&A, 1983
British Glass Between the Wars Exhibition Catalogue, Broadfield House Glass Museum, 1987
Bumpus, Bernard, *Charlotte Rhead – Potter and Designer*, 1987
Catley, Brian, *Art Deco and Other Figures*, 1978
Brunhammer, Yvonne, *The Nineteen Twenties Style*, 1966
Charleston, R.J., *World Ceramics*, 1990
Susie Cooper Productions, Exhibition Catalogue, V&A 1987
Cross, A.J., *Pilkingtons Royal Lancastrian Pottery and Tiler*, 1980
Dawes, Nicholas M., *Lalique Glass*, 1986
Decelle, Phillipe, *Sabino – Catalogue Raisonne*, 1987
The Delorenzo Gallery, *Jean Dunand*, New York 1985
Deutsche Keramik Des 20 Jahrhunderts, Catalogue of the Hetjens Museums; Dusseldorf, vols I and II, 1985
Dufrêne, Maurice, *Art Deco Interiors*, London
Duncan, Alastair, *American Art Deco*, 1986
Art Deco Furniture, 1984
Eyles, Desmond, *Doulton Burslem Wares*, 1980
Doulton Lambeth Wares, 1975
Eyles and Dennis, *Royal Doulton Figures*, 1978
Gabardi, Melissa, *Art Deco Jewellery*, 1989
Glass in Sweden 1915-1916, various authors, 1986
Goddens Encyclopedia of British Pottery and Porcelain Marks, 1978
Griffin, L. & Meisel, L.K. and S.P., *Clarice Cliff — The Bizarre Affair*, 1988
Hilschenz-Mlynek, Helga, and Ricke, Helmut, *Glass*, 1985
Hanks, David A., *The Decorative Designs by Frank Lloyd Wright*, 1979
Haslam, Malcolm, *Marks and Monograms of the Modern Movement 1875-1930*, 1977

Hayward, Helena, *World Furniture*, 1977
Hillier, Bevis, *Posters*, 1969
The World of Art Deco, 1971
Janneau, Guillaume, *Modern Glass*, 1931
Jones, Mark, *The Art of the Medal*, 1979
Klein, Dan, and Bishop, Margaret, *Decorative Art 1880-1980*, 1986
Klein, Dan, and Lloyd, Ward, *History of Glass*, 1988
Krekel-Aalberse, Annelies, *Art Nouveau and Art Deco Silver*, 1989
Kunst Diesich Nutzlichuch Macht, Industrial Design at the Neue Sammlung Museum, Munich, 1985
Lalique – A Century of Glass for a Modern World, Exhibition Catalogue
Lesieutre, Alain, *Art Deco*, 1974
Lipmann, Anthony, *Divinely Elegant – The World of Ernst Dryden*, 1989
Ludwig, Coy, *Maxfield Parrish*, 1973
Lukins, Jocelyn, *Doulton for the Collector*, 1989
Marcilhac, Felix, *R. Lalique – Catalogue Raisonne*, 1989
Mortimer, Tony L., *Lalique Jewellery and Glassware*, 1989
Opie, Jennifer, *Scandinavian Ceramics and Glass in the Twentieth Century*, 1989
Page, Marion *Furniture Designed by Architects*, 1980
Percy, C.V., *The Glass of Lalique*, 1977
Phaidon Encyclopaedia of Decorative Arts, edited by Phillipe Garner, 1978
Rutherford, Jessica and Beddoc, Stella, *Art Nouveau, Art Deco and the Thirties; the Ceramic, Glass and Metalwork Collections at Brighton Museum*, 1986
Schnessel, Michael S., *Icart*, 1976
Sembach, Leuthauser, Gossel, *Twentieth Century Furniture Design*, Cologne (not dated)
Stimpson, Miriam, *Modern Furniture Classic*, 1987
The Thirties, Exhibition Catalogue, The Hayward Gallery, 1979
Watson, *Collecting Clarice Cliff*, 1988
Wilk, Christopher, *Marcel Breuer – Furniture and Interiors*, 1981

INDEX

PICTURE CREDITS AND ACKNOWLEDGMENTS

The publishers would like to the thank the following auction houses, museums, dealers, collectors and other sources for kindly supplying pictures for use in this book or for allowing their pieces to be photographed.

10 CL; 12 SM; 13 SM; 14 SM; 15 SM; 16 CNY; 17 SM; 18 CNY; 19 CNY; 20 CL; 21 SM; 22 SM; 23 SM; 24 SL; 26 WF; 27l ND, 27r CNY; 28 CNY; 29 CNY; 30 CNY; 31 CNY; 32 SL; 33 CL; 34 CL; 35l CL, 35r SL; 36t P; 36b S; 37t S; 37lb CNY; 37br CL; 38 CNY; 40 B; 41(x2) SM; 42lt CNY, 42lb SL, 42r(x2) B; 43lt CNY, 43lb(x2) B, 43b,rt SL, 43 B; 44 CG; 45l CM, 45r B; 46 CM; 47 CNY; 48 CG; 49 CNY; 50 SM; 51(x2) SM; 52 B; 53(x2) B; 54 B; 55(x3) B; 56 SNY; 57l CNY, 57r B; 58 CG; 59l CG, 59r SNY; 60 SL; 61(x2) Cor; 62 B; 63t(x3) B, 63b(x2) NT; 64 B; 66 CNY; 67(x2) SL; 68 SM; 69t GM; 69b B; 70 CNY; 71 SNY; 72 B; 73(x3) B; 74 CL; 75(x2) CL; 76(x5) B; 77lt P, 77lb B, 77rb CL; 78 B; 80 B; 81(x3) B; 82 B; 83(x2) B; 84 B; 86 B; 87 B; 88 B; 89(x3) B; 90 B; 91(x2) B; 92 SL; 93l SL, 93r CL; 94 B; 96 CNY; 97 PB; 98 CNY; 99 MM; 100c B, 100b(x2) FG; 101lt B, 101lb B, 101rt NT; 101rb B; 103 CNY; 104 SM; 105 SM; 106 CNY; 107 CNY; 108 CNY; 109 CL; 110 SL; 111t SL, 111b CNY; 112 B; 113t CL, 113b CNY; 114 CNY; 115 SL; 116 CNY; 117 B; 118 HA; 119(x2) NM; 120 CL; 122 CNY; 123 CM; 124 B; 125 B; 126 P; 128 CNY; 129(x2) P; 130 CNY; 131 CNY; 132 CL; 133l CL; 133r CNY; 134 SNY; 135 SNY; 136 B; 137l B, 137rt SM, 137rb SM; 138 B; 139lt,lb B, 139rt,rb CS; 140 B; 141t(x2) CG, 141b B; 142 CNY; 144 CNY; 145 CNY; 146 CNY; 147 B; 148 CG; 149l CG, 149rt NT; 150 CNY; 151lt CNY, 151lb MG, 151r MG; 152t B, 152b CNY; 153 B; 154 B; 156 CNY; 157t CNY, 157b CL; 158 SNY; 160 CL; 161t SL, 161b SM; 162 WF; 163t CL, 163b B; 164 SL; 165l Col, 165rt,rc SM, 165rb SNY; 166 SG; 167lt SG, 167lb SM, 167r CG; 168 SNY; 169t CG, 169b SNY; 170(x3) B; 17lt(x3) SL; 171b(x2) NT; 172 CNY; 174 CNY; 175l SM, 175r SL; 176 SL; 177t SL, 177b V&A; 178t SM, 178lb SL, 178rb CSK; 179(x2) SL

KEY
b bottom, c centre, l left, r right, t top

B	Bonham's, London		Art, New York
CL	Christie's, London	ND	Nicholas M. Dawes,
CG	Christie's, Geneva		New York
CNY	Christie's, New York	NM	National Museum of
Col	Antique Collectors Club		American Art,
Cor	Corning Museum of		Smithsonian
	Glass, New York		Institution
CS	Charles Spencer	NT	Noel Tovey, L'Odeon
CSK	Christie's, South	P	Phillips, London
	Kensington	PB	Patricia Bayer
DDC	Donald and Diane	SL	Sotheby's, London
	Cameron	SM	Sotheby's, Monaco
FG	Frances Gertler	SNY	Sotheby's, New York
GM	Galerie Moderne	V&A	Victoria and Albert
HA	Hirschl & Adler Galleries,		Museum, London
	Inc., New York	WF	The Wolfsonian
MG	Maison Gerard, New York		Foundation, Miami,
MM	Metropolitan Museum of		Florida

Thanks are due to the following for their generous help in the preparation of this book:
Bob Lawrence, Gallery 25
Clive Stewart Lockhart
Noel Tovey

Special thanks are due to Nicholas Dawes for his invaluable contribution to the American sections of this book.